Settled
Wanderers

Sam Berkson
& Mohamed Sulaiman

Dear Joey,

Samuel Berkson

April 2015

Influx Press, London

Published by Influx Press

Office 3A, Mill Co Project. Unit 3, Gaunson House, Markfield Road
London. N15 4QQ
www.influxpress.com

First published 2015

Printed and bound in the UK by the Short Run Press Ltd, Exeter
ISBN 978-0-9927655-4-5

*Dedicated to the Saharawi people and their 40 year
struggle for self-determination.*

'nothing, however profitable, goes on forever'

– C. L. R. James, *The Black Jacobins*, 1938

Contents

Aminatou Haider - Saharawi activist

Introduction: The imperative of Western Saharan cultural resistance

A few years ago, a friend of ours, Carlos Gonzalez, directed a documentary film *Robbed of Truth*, about the conditions in the Western Saharan refugee camps in southwestern Algeria. These camps, which have been home to nearly one half of the native Western Saharan population since Morocco's invasion of their homeland in 1975, are a place where Western Saharan nationalism has thrived for three decades. And yet these camps also embody the failure of the international community to oppose Morocco's conquest and colonisation of Western Sahara. In *Robbed of Truth*, a Spanish relief worker with years of experience in those camps remarks on the chronic, and sometimes deadly, health problems the refugees face, having lived on emergency food aid for several decades. He provocatively concludes that what he has witnessed is the genocide of the Western Saharan people.

It is neither hyperbolic nor a stretch of the imagination to see the situation in Western Sahara as a genocide. It is not the kind of genocide we have come to expect, the kind where one ethnic group rapidly exterminates another group through mass killings. It is a slow genocide based on political identities, one conducted over the course of four decades by the Moroccan regime against the Western Saharan nation, with the tacit complicity of the United Nations Security Council all along the way.

The UN Convention on the Prevention and Punishment of the Crime of Genocide provides the authoritative international definition of genocide. Among the acts the convention recognises as genocidal are those that attempt the following: 'Deliberately inflicting on the group conditions of life calculated to bring about its physical destruction in whole or in part.' Groups who can be subjected to genocide include those of 'national, ethnical, racial or religious' character. Since invading the Spanish administered Western Sahara in 1975, this is exactly what the Kingdom of Morocco has attempted to do — to suppress and ultimately eradicate Western Saharan nationalism. But instead of its physical destruction, Moroccan policies have aimed at the symbolic erasure of the Western Saharan nation. This has occurred not only through the longstanding denial of the territory's right to self-determination but, more importantly, through Morocco's strategies of colonisation, which have sought to envelop Western Sahara into Morocco territorially, culturally, architecturally, economically, administratively, and, of course, politically. The genocide of the Western Saharan nation is at once obvious just as it is insidious.

Given this reality, celebrations of Western Saharan culture and identity — like those in this collection, *Settled Wanderers* —

serve to remind us of Western Saharan nationalism's continued existence against the powerful forces of geopolitics. However the poems in this collection are also part of the struggle against those forces, the fight against the prolonged yet ambiguous genocide of the Western Saharan nation. What we would like to do in this brief introductory essay is describe the emergence of Western Saharan nationalism and the geopolitical forces it has had to contend with, so that the importance of Western Saharan cultural resistance is underscored.

From colony to nation

Like much of continent, the territory of Western Sahara was claimed in that desperate land grab known as the Scramble for Africa of the 1880s. What distinguished Western Sahara from its neighbours was the colonising power, Spain. By then, Spain was a faded European power eclipsed by France, Great Britain, and Germany, controlling only a tiny enclave and a couple islands in Africa's equatorial regions and, in the northwestern part of the continent, the desert region we now know as Western Sahara and the volcanic archipelago offshore. Madrid's only interest in the territory was securing the rich fishing grounds between the African coast and the Canary Islands, which Spain had conquered in the fifteenth century. With the definitive boundaries of the territory established in 1912, the Western Sahara was an Iberian aberration in a sea of French dominion: the colonies of Algeria to the east and French West Africa to the south, and then Franco-Spanish protectorate of Morocco to the north.

For the people of Western Sahara, living primarily as pastoralist nomads, these new borders were not consistent with any natural, social, or political geography that they recognised. Nor was there an intense Spanish effort to colonise the territory and 'civilise' the natives until after WWII when rich phosphate deposits were discovered in Western Sahara, thereby requiring labour and security. The Western Saharans are often called, and call themselves, Saharawis. Though there is a temptation to see the Saharawi identity as a pre-colonial ethnic identity, the territory of Western Sahara is at the heart of the Saharawi identity. That is to say, Saharawis, in the broadest sense, are Hassaniyah speaking peoples who claim membership in one of the 'tribes' whose traditional range included the territory of Spanish Sahara. Thus the territory and the identity are inextricably linked, though it is possible to speak of Moroccan and Algerian Saharawis too. More importantly, the invention of the Saharawi identity — Arabic for Saharan — was an act of linguistic resistance: the native Western Saharans were not Spanish Saharan, they were simply Saharans.

The geographical elaboration of the Western Saharan nation-state was enhanced by Spanish efforts to make the territory a viable colony, albeit very late in the game. By the 1950s, it was clear that the age of European colonialism was coming to an end, and yet Spain was only just getting started in Western Sahara: making significant investments in the territory, settling the population, and engaging some Western Saharans in government and the security sector. Yet the war for Algerian independence, which began in 1954, and the restoration of Moroccan self-rule in 1956 encouraged Western Saharans to rise up against Spain in 1957. French soldiers in Algeria and French West Africa aided the counterinsurgency campaign. The Hispano-French response was, according to historical accounts, brutal; several thousand Western Saharans fled to the relative safety of southern Morocco, which would become the incubator for a new nationalist movement over a decade later.

Spain held on to Western Sahara long after Algeria won its independence in 1962, two years after French West Africa dissolved into the states of the western Sahel — notably Mauritania, Mali, and Niger. Though increasingly subjected to demands from the United Nations to provide Western Sahara with self-determination and, by the early 1970s, outright independence, Madrid instead cultivated a local elite that would perpetuate its rule there. Upon their independence, Morocco and Mauritania had launched challenges to Spanish colonialism in Western Sahara, raising claims on the territory and its people. It was in this context that a new Western

Saharan independence movement emerged, one neither aligned with Spanish neocolonial interests nor with Moroccan and Mauritanian irredentism. Founded in 1973, the Polisario Front quickly earned international recognition as the most popular political movement in Western Sahara when the United Nations visited the territory in the summer of 1975.

By that time, Spain had already signaled its intent to hold a referendum on independence. Morocco and Mauritania, recognising the power of the Western Saharan independence movement, sought to block Spain from holding the vote by putting the issue before the International Court of Justice. When the World Court examined Morocco and Mauritania's claims, it found no credible evidence of either state having had sovereignty over Western Sahara. Despite this opinion, Morocco quickly announced plans to invade the territory in mid October 1975. As Morocco was a close ally of the United States in the Cold War, US officials made sure the Security Council did not oppose Morocco's conquest. Rather than risk a war, Spain opted to hand the territory over to Morocco and Mauritania. The Western Saharan independence movement, by then supported by Algeria and initially by Libya, focused its efforts on helping support the thousands of refugees fleeing the invading troops.

From war to "peace"

The geopolitics of the Cold War allowed Morocco to take Western Sahara and the same geopolitics allowed Morocco to keep it. As is often the case when foreign armies occupy territories and peoples they know little about, the Mauritanians and Moroccans were often routed by Polisario's guerrillas. Indeed, Mauritania was soon driven out of Western Sahara. Facing the prospect of defeat in Western Sahara, Morocco used the Cold War to gain substantial military and political support from Washington and Paris, as well as financial support from Saudi Arabia. Morocco's counterinsurgency strategy centered on the construction of a series of defensive walls dug out of the desert. These heavily mined and intensively patrolled 'berms' expanded from the northwest to the east and the south of the territory. By 1987, the final wall — snaking from the Atlantic Ocean near the Mauritanian border to the Algerian frontier in southern Morocco — represented one of the most fortified defensive lines in the world. Today Western Saharans often call it the wall of shame, for it represents the continued and enforced division of the Western Saharans into an occupied population and an exiled one.

With military victory ruled out for both sides, Morocco and Polisario began working with the United Nations in the late 1980s to solve the issue. Morocco had ostensibly committed itself to a referendum, though this was an ambiguous commitment. Indeed, the UN Security Council created the UN Mission for the Referendum in Western Sahara (MINURSO) in 1991, only to see the mission become mired in Moroccan efforts to flood the electorate with Moroccans posing as Western Saharans. It took the UN mission five years to sort through over 240,000 voter candidates, arriving at a list of only 86,000. The vast majority of those rejected had been sponsored by Morocco. Having failed to rig the referendum, Morocco's new King, Mohammed VI, who came to power in mid 1999, reneged on his late father's commitment to an independence referendum. In late 1999, the United States and France were also in no mood to test Morocco's young king with an independence referendum in Western Sahara. Indeed, the Security Council had recently learned a bitter lesson when it failed to anticipate the obvious: the bloody wrath of Indonesia's security forces when East Timor's 1999 self-determination referendum resulted in a vote for independence. In early 2000, Morocco's allies on the Security Council essentially abandoned the independence referendum that the United Nations had spent the last decade attempting to organize.

For roughly twenty years (1981-2001), the Western Sahara peace process was based on a weak but clear consensus between Morocco and the nationalist movement: the fate of Western Sahara would be decided by a vote. This consensus was also consistent with international law, as the UN Secretariat has acknowledged that the United Nations cannot be part of a peace process that does not allow Africa's last non-self-governing territory a vote on independence. So when France and the United States allowed Morocco to back away from its commitment to such a vote, the Security Council became complicit in undermining what little progress had been made towards peace in Western Sahara since the African Union (then the OAU) secured Morocco's commitment to a vote in the early 1980s. Little surprise, then, that the Western Sahara peace process has made little progress in the past decade and a half. Polisario demands a referendum on independence; Morocco rejects it. Morocco wants Polisario to accept limited autonomy under Moroccan rule as the sole basis for negotiations; Polisario wants Morocco to accept a referendum as a pre-condition for serious talks.

Given the paralysis of the international diplomacy to settle the Western Sahara conflict, Western Saharan nationalists, particularly those in the Moroccan occupied territory, increasingly turned to nonviolent resistance to challenge both Rabat's harsh policies and the international indifference to their plight. Small scale protests in the late 1980s and early 1990s were often met with brutal reprisals from the occupying authorities. Then, in 1999, a group of Saharawi students decided to test the new king of Morocco on his claims to be a champion of human rights and the poor. A large protest camp in the middle of the largest city, L'Ayoune, was formed, representing various tendencies within Western Saharan civil society. As the camp grew, so did the protestors claims, shifting from civil rights to the right of self-determination. The Moroccan crackdown was harsh, enlisting local gangs of Moroccan settlers to their aid. Soon protests became more frequent and daring. The Western Saharan rights movement, once small and heavily repressed, grew into a powerful movement. Significant demonstrations in 2005 forced the UN Secretariat to re-engage the stalled peace process.

Out of the 2005 protests, new faces of Western Saharan nationalism began to speak to people abroad about the daily suffering and struggles of the Saharawis under Moroccan rule. Aminatou Haidar, one of the most prominent, began winning a series of international human rights awards in Europe and North America. Then, in late 2010, mere months before the Arab Spring would seemingly erupt in Tunisia, Western Saharans staged an ingenious form of protest: they established their own refugee camp in the desert outside L'Ayoune. This camp not only served to voice Saharawis feelings of second-class political and economic status in Morocco, it also showed solidarity with the long suffering Western Saharan refugees in Algeria. The Gdeim Izik camp, as it would come to be known, soon had over 10,000 inhabitants. In a rebuke to the Moroccan occupation, the camp suggested that for Western Saharans to be free, they had to be refugees. Moroccan authorities nonetheless used the Gdeim Izik as an excuse to crack down on the Western Sahara human rights movement, imprisoning some of its most important members on questionable yet serious charges. Events such as these only continue to convince the Western Saharan refugees that armed struggle is their only option to achieve self-determination.

Conclusion

As the Arab Spring began, the media quickly forgot about the events in Western Sahara. Morocco itself emerged from the Arab Spring with its regime intact, having promised reforms and more power sharing. In a region beset by instability (Libya and Mali) and uncertainty (Algeria and Tunisia), North Atlantic powers once again looked to Morocco as a bulwark of stability. The cost of this 'stability' was paid by the people of Western Sahara, who continue to live in exile in Algeria or under one of the most repressive police states in the world. The Western Sahara peace process has, since the Arab Spring, become even more dysfunctional, as Morocco — ever confident in its support from Washington and Paris — has become increasingly unresponsive to UN mediation efforts.

That said, Moroccan occupation authorities and Moroccan settlers quietly acknowledge that the overwhelming majority of Saharawis want independence and that their control of the territory remains based primarily on force. Although the Moroccan autonomy plan for the territory certainly does not meaningfully address Morocco's legal responsibility to recognize the Saharawi's right of self-determination, it nevertheless constitutes a reversal of Morocco's historical insistence that Western Sahara is as much a part of Morocco as other provinces by acknowledging that Western Sahara is indeed a distinct entity. Meanwhile, protests in Western Sahara in recent years have begun to raise some awareness within Morocco, especially among intellectuals, human rights activists, pro-democracy groups, and some moderate Islamists — long suspicious of the government line in a number of areas — that not all Saharawis see themselves as Moroccans and that there exists a genuine indigenous opposition to Moroccan control.

The Moroccan government has spent nearly four decades and billions of dollars to occupy, colonize, and transform Western Sahara. Though these efforts to 'Moroccanise' the territory and the Sahrawis are essentially a genocide against the Western Saharan nation, they have so far not succeeded. Western Saharan resistance and transnational support for it show no sign of acquiescing to Morocco's attempts at a fait accompli. The enormous worldwide success of Saharawi musician Aziza Brahim is just one of the most prominent, recent demonstrations of the sublime power of Western Saharan cultural resistance.

In the occupied territory and the refugee camps, even the most quotidian acts — Saharawi cultural celebrations or the wearing traditional clothing — have become forms of resistance that some activists refer to as 'the silent protests.' Efforts to preserve and promote Saharawi culture manifest in underground schools that teach Saharawi children in their Hassaniyah dialect of Arabic and Spanish, rather than the Moroccan Arabic and French used in Moroccan schools. Despite the fact that Polisario's leadership has lived in exile, separated from the majority of the population for over three decades, a new generation of Western Saharan nationalists, who have known only Moroccan occupation their entire lives, are finding new ways and new outlets for promoting traditional and hybrid forms of Saharawi culture amongst themselves and to the world via the internet.

The perseverance of Saharawi culture, including its rich tradition of poetry, has played a critical role in keeping the struggle for self-determination alive, despite enormous odds. This collection underscores how the power of cultural identity, including the spoken word, can challenge the intrigues of foreign powers.

— Jacob Mundy & Stephen Zunes, 2015

An Analysis of Saharawi Folk Poetry

The analysis and appreciation of Sahrawi folk poetry used to be a predominantly subjective thing, and it was only very recently that it began to be the subject of rigorous research. For this reason, it is extremely difficult to pinpoint the date of the emergence of Saharawi folk poetry, although a large number of researchers suggest that it reached its zenith in the twelfth century.

As a human creative expression, Sahrawi poetry evolved over the centuries in tandem with the evolution of the Sahrawi society itself. Musical and rhythmic poetic modes were developed to express a variety of emotional situations, be they joy, heroism, longing, sadness or nostalgia. Over time, folk poetry evolved into refined and diverse poetic genres associated with wisdom, mysticism, praise, love and poetic contest.

As with any other form of poetic expression, Saharawi folk poetry has been the bearer of the local language of society, its culture, wisdom, values, folklore and mythology, and reflected the social mores of Saharawi society at every stage of its evolution. It has also served as a tool of communication and active interaction with other societies.

Hassaniya-speaking society is a society that delights in poetry, which is widely appreciated across genders and ages. Given the association in the collective imagination between poetry and singing, both poets and reciters of poetry are highly respected in the community. Their art is known in Hassaniya as *leghna* (singing or lyric poetry), even if they do not use musical instruments in their performance. For this reason, a poet is described as a *lemgani* in Hassaniya, and poetry is also called *almauzun*, which means something that is well measured or rhythmically balanced.

For a piece to be considered poetry and different from prose, it should fulfil a certain number of socially established criteria that poets have to observe. The first criterion is *al wazen*, meaning that there are rhymes at the ends of both the two half-lines (*teefelweet*, plural *teefelwatan*), in which each verse is composed. The second condition relates to the metre, the measuring unit of which being the stanza (*ghaf*) or poem (*talaa*). The type of vowels used in each half-line determines the basic metrical units and metres of Saharawi poetry.

Saharawi folk poetry has played a prominent role in the different aspects of Saharawi life, especially during the course of the struggle waged by the Saharawi people for self-determination. Saharawi poets, who have been at the forefront of the struggle, have produced works that sought to alleviate the suffering and face up to adversities, preaching victory and paying tribute to the tremendous sacrifices made by their fellows in the fight for freedom and dignity.

A significant contribution of Saharawi verse consists in its introduction into the Hassaniya-speaking world of a new genre: socially committed poetry. This type of poetry is characterised by its clear and sustained commitment to the cause and the struggle of the people, expressed poetically and appraised from different perspectives. Because of its fluent, direct and rhetorical character, socially committed poetry has also played a pedagogical role, teaching the community the great values and philosophy of the revolution underway, thus contributing significantly to the ongoing social changes. Moreover, by infusing standard Arabic into its *guifan* (plural of *gaf*, stanza), Saharawi poetry has contributed to bringing this 'high' language closer to the community, while elevating Hassaniya dialect to the level of standard Arabic.

In view of the limited means of communication in a vast desert environment, socially committed poetry has also played a complementary role in furthering (and sometimes even challenging) the political discourse and transmitting its message to a wider audience, both in the refugee camps as well as in the Moroccan-occupied territories and across the diaspora.

Hassaniya-speaking poetry as a whole has also evolved in tandem with the evolution of the Saharawi society and the exigencies of modern life where it can be seen used, for instance, in advertisements and election campaigns, among other places. Its vocabulary has been enriched by loanwords, especially technical terms taken from different languages such as bus, telephone, taxi, *marché*, and so forth.

The traditional modes regulating the transmission and reception of poetry have also evolved in tandem with the needs of modern life and the introduction of new technologies such as radio, television and the internet. However, the oral character of Saharawi poetry and the immediacy of its transmission and reception in private and in public ceremonies and festivals have still been preserved.

It is noteworthy that the evolution of Saharawi folk poetry has taken place in an unique situation in which the Saharawi people are divided between the refugee camps and the Moroccan-occupied territories. Thousands of Saharawis have been living in refugee camps for almost forty years owing to the Moroccan military invasion and the subsequent annexation of their territory. For these people, poetry has been a mobilising and driving force in their struggle to preserve their culture and heritage and to assert their cultural distinctiveness and political independence. Meanwhile, thousands of other Saharawis continue to live in Moroccan-occupied Western Sahara. They are subjected to repression, abuse, imprisonment, abduction as well as enforced 'disappearance' on a daily basis. For these people, poetry has been a central tool in their resistance to occupation and a major medium for voicing their grievances and demands and for preserving their cultural heritage and identity.

- Mustafa El-Kattab, January 2015
(translated by M. Limam Mohamed Ali)

Translatation and Interpretation of Saharawi poetry

This book is not a comprehensive study of Western Saharan poetry. It is a record of my experience of the Saharawi refugee camps and my understanding of the poetry I heard.

I visited the camps twice, each time for about two weeks, once in November, in the brief period when the nights are cool but not too cold and the daytimes hot but not impossible, making a climate pleasant enough for the flies to flourish in astonishing numbers and to create the 'sickness season'. The next time was in May when the real heat is just beginning and I glimpsed what life must be like in the extreme summer heat of the Earth's hottest desert. Originally I travelled out with Olive Branch as one of two documentary artists (photographer Emma Brown was the other) following the London charity as they helped young people on the camps devise and stage a piece of theatre. While I was there, I asked to meet local poets and I was introduced to three: Hussein Ma'aloud, Beyibouh Al Haj and Al Khadra Mabrook. Zorgan Laroussi, Chaka Mohamed and Lejilfa Mahmud, on top of their tireless work interpreting for Olive Branch around the camps, helped me translate a poem from each of them. I also wrote some poems of my own.

Later when discussing ideas for a new book with my editor, Kit Caless at Influx Press, I suggested – as one outside possibility among others – returning to the camps and writing some more. This, to my surprise, was the option that Kit was interested in. With the advice of Becky Finlay Hall at Olive Branch, we set up a crowd funding project and raised enough money to send me back again.

Sidi Breika and Limam Mohamed are the Polisario Mission to the UK: the non-official ambassadors of a non-recognised government-in-exile. They were extremely helpful, arranging things at last minute and efficiently setting me up with everything I would need on the camps. I was to stay again with Zorgan and his wife, Mimi. A young man with a degree in English Literature by the name of Mohamed Sulaiman was to be my translator. As luck would have it, it turned out he was also an illustrator and he would be able to provide some pen and ink drawings and calligraphy for the book. The Polisario Ministry of Culture were supportive throughout, and it was they who arranged meetings with the poets.

So I returned to the camps, this time on my own and with a voice recorder. It was a pretty tight schedule and we were not able to translate all of the poems we recorded. The book's selection is mainly circumstantial and some poets missed out more than others, depending on which point in the trip we met them. Thus, though I have recordings of more, there are only two Al Khadra pieces and one from Hadjatu Aliat Swelm in the book, meaning that women's voice weighs even less in this book than it should do. When – God or whoever else willing – I return again, I hope to find time with Mohamed to translate them.

The translation method quickly established itself. I would meet the poet, talk to her or him. Once s/he sufficiently understood me and was comfortable with what I was doing, they would recite something for me. That was my first contact with the poem. I would hear it, record it and watch the poet as s/he said it. Mohamed would give me a brief synopsis of what had been said. The poet might recite some more for me.

Later, at Mimi and Zorgan's home, Mohamed listened back to the poems, painstakingly writing the words down, going back over each line to check his transcription. When he had finished, we would play it back in its entirety. For him, this acted as one final check of the accuracy. For me, there was a chance to hear the poem again as it was performed. We would then go through it, word-for-word, trying to establish as literal a translation as possible, trying to understand its meaning.

I would ask annoying questions:

'What does it say literally? Which word means "leader" in that line?' 'Where else would you use that word?' 'Does it sound like a positive thing?'

'How formal a title is that?'

I was looking to understand what the poem meant to Mohamed, what it meant to a native speaker who knew the language and the literature well.

Mohamed would ask me questions too:

'What verb would you use for something that is hurting, but not just as you feel it in the moment, but continuing to hurt?' We would discuss the appropriateness of my suggestions.

Eventually, we would have a draft of a fairly literal translation, splattered with asterisks, footnotes, transliterations in Roman alphabet, alternative readings. Back in England, I tried to find the right voice for each poem.

There seems to be roughly two polar approaches to translation. There is the Nabokov theory – that although, 'the expression "a literal translation" is more or less nonsense', translation should be an act of 'mimicry'. He declared that: 'The worst, degree of turpitude is reached when a masterpiece is planished and patted into such a shape, vilely beautified in such a fashion as to conform to the notions and prejudices of a given public. This is a crime, to be punished by the stocks as plagiarists were in the shoebuckle days.'

Others would argue that this is precisely the only way to translate something. Literal translation is impossible, the 'essence' of the text must be recomposed and reworked completely. The rebels against Nabokov's laws might argue that a translator, particularly of poetry, should indeed planish, pat and beautify so that a speaker of one tongue, with one set of prejudices, will hear the translated poem with the same feeling as a speaker of the original language, with her own (non-translatable) notions and prejudices.

Inspired not a little by Christopher Logue's renditions of 'The Iliad', I thought I might do something closer to the latter. Just as he did not know Greek and was no specialist in classical culture, neither did I know Hassaniya and was an outsider to Saharawi culture, relying on interpreters and experts to help me through. However, as in most endeavours, method is established through practice. In the end, each poem decided for me how I would approach it. Throwing away both Nabokov and Logue, I refer you to the architect Louis Kahn: 'You say to a brick, "What do you want, brick?" And brick says to you, "I like an arch." And you say to brick, "Look, I want one, too, but arches are expensive and I can use a concrete lintel." And then you say: "What do you think of that, brick?" Brick says: "I like an arch."'

Those proficient in both languages can judge the faithfulness of my translation and the rest of you must judge each poem as I have produced it, not its relation to the original. If my method is successful you should hear the voice of the distant poet speaking to you in my voice (or perhaps my voice speaking in the voice of another), the poem declaring itself in a language beyond the Babelian systems which divide us.

All of the Hassaniya poems are composed in strict rhyme and metrical patterns, but what would be the point of trying to reproduce those patterns in a language which has different sounds and different rhythms? Some poems seemed forthright or funny and for them rhyme seemed appropriate; others were sad or reflective and for them I used slower, more diffuse free verse, though free verse does not exist in Saharawi poetry.

Sometimes I have kept transliterated versions of the original words. Dreimissa, for instance, I have kept as such. Dreimissa – 'a hornless goat' – is the common name for a pickup-type 1960s Land Rover with its cabin stripped away and a gun mounted in the back: an improvised tank for a guerrilla army. In the explanatory sub-heading and within the poem's first few lines, I have tried to give you a few alternative renderings, but essentially the word, to people who have long ago forgotten goatherding and whose army are one of the most expensively equipped in the world, is untranslatable. At other times there is a footnote, but as much as possible I tried to make the poems 'speak for themselves' without too much additional explanation.

'Dreimissa' in its original starts with some puns with numbers; something to do with the designation or the serial number of the Land Rover. I could barely follow the explanation, let alone translate it. Instead, I begin with an acrostic. I hope it conveys a similarly light-hearted, celebratory ode-to-the-Land-Rover start to the poem. Some poems needed more adjusting than others. Long praise poems detailing the qualities of a Saharawi hero, such as Bashir Ali's 'Bassiri', are made exciting to listen to in the original by the rhyming and by the collective feeling they inspire for those who also wish to celebrate those imprisoned or murdered heroes. In English, translated too literally, they might sound like a list of adjectives and foreign names. At other times, little in the way of rearranging or gloss is needed; how powerful it is to hear Badi long for Norashin and Tingaphouf!

These translations, you might say, are my interpretations of Mohamed's translations. The essence of them might not be familiar to an English language poetry reader. I am sure that a creative writing tutor would tell the Saharawi poets to make their work less preachy and partisan, informing them that artists should ask questions and seek only to depict the truth as they subjectively see it. The Saharawi poems in this book are different and varied but they are often directly and boldly political. They believe in certain objective realities and sometimes have more in common with the poetics of Chuck D than with Seamus Heaney or Carol Ann Duffy. Perhaps some English critics will be put off by that.

However, most of these critics have not had direct experience of war. The war in Western Sahara was immediate and urgent, the irresolution of its aftermath bitter and long-lasting. It involved everyone. In the camps, almost all able-bodied men were mobilised. Women became builders, ran the institutions, smuggled arms, provided intelligence; they were radio operators, drivers, spies or medics. These poems mirror a resistance that is remarkably collective and non-violent given the fracturing of the people and what they have endured in the forty years since the Moroccan invasion.

***

It was mid-afternoon at Chaka's house. It was hot. We had eaten chicken, prepared and served by Chaka's wife. Chaka, Mohamed, Bendir the driver and myself all lay down on the floor of the room to sleep, our heads resting on hard cushions, each finding a spot near one of the windows to catch any cooling breeze that the baking hot afternoon could afford us. As I began to drift off, my phone rang. It was the BBC. A researcher wanted to know what I thought about Jeremy Paxman saying that modern poetry is irrelevant. He would like to invite me to discuss it. I drowsily stumbled outside into the unforgiving glare of hot desert sun and tried to explain that I was away in Algeria where I had just met Al-Khadra, who at seventy-five years old, was still composing poems. This woman, hardened by forty years of refugee camps and struggle, had told me only a few hours earlier: 'All my poems are for the revolution.'

Of course poetry can be relevant. What is it that makes a personal experience collective? In war, perhaps, it is obvious. One veteran of the Polisario army (you will meet him in 'Particulars') told me his regiment had one Kalashnikov between six soldiers. Moroccan planes bombed the territory before it could ever become Western Sahara. Tanks rolled in. Towns were looted and pillaged. Bodies were dumped in mass graves in the desert. And yet, the Polisario arranged for tens of thousands to be evacuated to safe space over the Algerian border. One billion dollars (in thirty-years-ago money) of military aid filled Morocco's coffers in five years. Against such odds, with what could a small, largely volunteer army fight, except ideas and principles? And about what else could poets speak ?

For sixteen years the Polisario were undefeated though unsuccessful. Mauritania were forced to withdraw their claim but Morocco could not be pushed back. Despite successive talks and U.N ambassadors, no referendum on independence was forthcoming. Repressed in the homeland or subsisting on 'emergency' food aid in exile, how do you maintain your hope and your dignity? And about what else then could poets speak?

***

Pub quiz question: Which oppressed Muslim people are said by some to have started the Arab Spring with a non-violent, month-long tented occupation in defiance of an authoritarian government? Answer: The Saharawi [c.f. Noam Chomsky, Gdeim Izik, Morocco]. This unique culture, made of (among other things) Bedouin hospitality, religious consideration of the right to life, democratic institutions, near universal literacy and women's rights, is not allowed to form itself as a nation.

***

This book is not anti-Moroccan. What kind of British hypocrite would that make me? It is in solidarity with everyone everywhere who is struggling for a better world. I would like Western readers to enjoy the poems and through appreciating them, consider the universality of art and humanity. But also I would like you to reflect on what it means to be subject to foreign occupation and to remember that your publically funded army also occupies foreign lands. Read these poems and remember that it is not just Saharawi who long for a country that does not exist yet. My sympathies are with Paxman having to wade through his pile of entries for the Forward Prize, despairing over poems about bowls of fruit and the light that falls on the hydrangeas. We must not forget that there are always pressing and relevant subjects. And to those creative writing tutors of objectivity and apolitical art, reflect if you can on the feeling of singing together of a future Jerusalem, built with mental strife and actual swords, in this green and pleasant land. I hope there will also be some who revel in poet-of-the-rifle Al Khadra's joy, watching the unveiling of the Polisario's first tank.

- Sam Berkson, London 2015.

PART ONE

Hassaniya poems interpreted to English

Gdeim Izik

"The Arab Spring began in November 2010 when the people of Western Sahara revolted against their Moroccan occupiers. The uprising was crushed by Moroccan troops"
- Noam Chomsky, lecture, University of Gaza, 2012

In 2010, a protest began when Saharawi activists from inside the Occupied Territories left the capital L'Ayoune and set up a tented protest camp on Gdeim Izik hill, just outside the city. The protest attracted up to twelve thousand people and lasted a month until it was shut down by Moroccan forces. Tents were burnt, eleven people killed, hundreds injured and many were arrested. Following the camp's eviction, violence and rioting spread to L'Ayoune which was eventually suppressed. Twenty three people are still held without charge in Sale jail.

Gdeim Izik
by Hossein Mo'ulud

The living land of Gdeim hill
and the unmovable resolution of the people´s will:
each of them completes the other,
reacts with the other,
and a flame leaps
as magnesium burns brilliantly in the air.
Together there is power.
How can you not see it there?

We accept without question
that the people's will is strong, and strengthening.
And we know that Gdeim will remain a symbol
of the hope of life and the invader's fear,
just as we are sure of what we see
when goodness or truth appears.

They walk tall in Gdeim, it's true.

The will runs deep in the marrow of our bones;

something the enemy can never make their own.

There, in Gdeim,

the tents that crown the hill

are braided with the threads of victory

from the tops of their poles

to the ground which they are based on,

where they stand as a giant in front of all creation.

The steps they took

shook regimes across the region

for all to see,

in front of all creation;

and the spirit emanates from Western Sahara:

from the hill of Gdeim,

down from the twin peaks of Mount Segain

and along Loren's long, flat plain.

To the Activists of Gdeim Izik
by Nadgem Said

In the grip of the King of Morocco's suppression
the revolutionaries showed strong against oppression,
free in thought, action and manner
and the flags that flew at Gdeim Izik
were freedom's proud banner.

They became themselves at Gdeim Izik;
Morocco ordered in the tear gas
and the truncheon stick.

The King thundered his sentences of death and of life
and the world that witnessed it
was horrified.

They saw the true face of that gangster king,
Monkey VI, whose army stole our land
and then walled us in.
What right has he to take them to court?
He, an usurper of conquest and war;

they, who struck camp
on land their ancestors walked.

Smuggled activists from abroad recorded what they saw;
witnessed Morocco was not righteous enough
to judge hearts selfless for the cause.

It is tyranny.
All he knows is violent prohibition,
military courts and extraordinary rendition.
Their stand shone in the light of revolution:
Our *haima*, holding our hill, defying exclusion,
Morocco's response can only embarrass him,
with our *intifada* there is no comparison.

In the grip of the King's suppression
the revolutionaries showed strong against oppression,
flouting his laws in freedom's true manner,
flying the colours of liberation's banner.

Gdeim Izik
by Hadjatu Aliat

The people of Gdeim Izik
sacrificed everything they might
disgracing the invader
with resistance that showed wrong from right.

The thunder clapped in the Four Cities
and a storm broke in the stronghold of the enemy.
The people's commitment hardened again
and you know that it was strong already!

The Saharawi youth harvested the fruit
that their mothers and fathers had planted,

taking up new tools for the struggle

that their elders had sparked in the first years of our hardship;

promising the enemy once again,

in displays of dauntless determination,

that the victory will be ours – a hope we've never hidden –

to be a free people in a state of our making.

The people of Gdeim Izik

sacrificed everything they might

until they had disgraced the invader

with a resistance that showed wrong from right.

Haima[1]
by Hossein Mo'ulud

Those ever open tents,

large and cooling dark:

their generous shade

and happy hearth

a haven for the helpless

a hostel for the traveller.

Sometimes a lone friendly outpost,

sometimes standing together,

they hold the heights of a little hill

or cluster on the soft cheek of a valley

where the plants mark the line of a dead river still.

Or as they are now in the Tindouf camps,

a living memorial of the struggle to survive

still open, still together

though exiled and divided from the land;

a refuge for those whose homes

were crushed under the tyrant's hand.

---

1. Since the Gdeim Izik protests, a banned object in occupied Western Sahara

Or as they are again now

back under the eyes of Morocco's conqueror king

whose hollow victory is haunted

by their remaining in Gdeim Izik.

Great that scene is!

Not hiding their heritage

but hollering their will:

these are the *haima* that the people should build.

You, Saharawi
by Hossein Mo'ulud

(written on the occasion of the launch of the campaign for those Gdeim Izik activists who are sentenced to life in prison)

You, Saharawi, strive and work

and never shirk to condemn

the invaders' injustice.

You press your rejection

into the hand that keeps its grip

over our land

and insist on that rejection

unfailingly;

an absolute rejection

in the words of our mouth

and the meditation of our hearts.

You refuse to kneel

or contract your thoughts

to the size of a king-stamped coin,

and thus sell out all that is yours.

The word of your promise is pure

and you have earned

your respect among great people.

From your earliest days
you wouldn't accept the
status of subject,
and we need not fear false whispers
of your surrender.

They threaten you;
you are not afraid of that.
They threaten you with years in prison,
they threaten you with life sentences,
or even a sentence that will send you to death;
tell them, *I want that and I am proud.*
My people reject you completely.

Remember, in the battle,
(as has often been repeated)
the soldier on the front line
who still has comrades behind
is never yet defeated.

Be with them!
by Bashir Ali

'The 'Gdeim Izik 25' were sentenced to long prison terms by a Moroccan military court on the basis of confessions obtained under torture.' – Report of the British Parliamentary Delegation to Western Sahara, February 2014.

.

Bright in the night they shine with good omens,

Titans of this life and in the next one, Trojans,

revolutionaries in our affection,

determined, ambitious and true to their intentions.

Heroes who held steadfast to their incorruptible aims,

overcame the oppressors and their underhand ways;

so firm in belief, they left no room for doubt,

they flaunted their freedom and let flags flout

the Moroccan-made, malicious laws,

caring for nothing but the goal of our cause,

battered by catastrophe but never giving in,

let the Lord reward them with all the good things,

and grant us the victory their courage deserves,

they presented their will and their proofs to the world.

There's no place on earth that has not been fanned

by flames that spread from the spark of their stand,

darkly suppressed by the enemy's hand:

an oppressor who refuses to consider them equal

insulting the glory of the indigenous people,

but they are in the land as the land is in them,
they accept their lot might be martyrdom,
if you can see this then you'll be with them!
If you know this is true
then you'll be with them!
Spare nothing that can help
and be with them!

Be with them.
Be with these hard-pressed heroes of hope,
tested by torture, bent but never broke.
Beaten and cuffed and threatened with killing,
They tried to force confessions but they were not willing
to destroy our unity as the enemy hoped that they would,
they broke the siege on our homeland and we say, 'that's good!'
They stand apart because they saw what seemed far away
and worked to bring it closer in a way
that caught the world mood,
saying, 'we stand opposed to your brutal attitude.'

So they left L'Ayoune and set up on their own
and people came to water the seeds that they'd sown,
stirred by the scenes they had witnessed
they furthered the reach of righteous resistance,
violence and terror made them stronger again,
it's my firm opinion that you should
be with them!
If you can hear what I'm saying you should
be with them!
They are good and resolute and you must
be with them!

Be with them,
because their intention was right,
oppression only elevated their level of fight,
and they lessened our affliction
with the best of convictions
that all empires have passed since the fall of Rome,
and they pinned their hearts to the call of home,
showed they weren't afraid of
prison or danger
because what they're made of
        is a persistent belief:

they're consistent indeed

to the existent need

to set the people free.

So when the enemy in vain tried to pay them off,

their integrity remained unstained and unsquashed,

because their word is one we know to trust

we know they'll never turn their backs on us.

Their honour is immaculate,

more generous than Hatam and just as passionate

for glory,

wrapping up a story

where the heartfelt feeling

rhymes with its reason

they seized the moment and the moment couldn't seize them

but Morocco locked them up and still hasn't freed them

and so you must

Be with them!

Heroes of the protest, I say

Be with them!

it would be *haram* to forget them and not

Be with them!

My advice to you as well as to them,

if you've got a clear conscience then,

Be with them!

WAR

'I say this: when we fought for independence, it was not money that did the fighting: it was love. Love for Kenya, our country, was what gave our young men courage to face the prospect of being mowed down by enemy bullets – and they would not let go of the soil.'

- Ngugi wa Thiong'o, *Devil on the Cross*, 1982

Dreimissa (ode to the Land Rover)
by Beyibouh El-Haj

In the war against Morocco, before the ELPS had tanks, Western Saharan fighters used the reconditioned Land Rover, which was popularly known as the 'Dreimissa' – literally, 'hornless goat'.

Light

And

Nimble,

Drives

Right

Over

Virtually

Every

Restriction.

Dreimissa!

Hornless goat,

topless landrover,

sawn-off shotgun loaded

with the bullets of liberation –

this song is for you,

for the fate that gave you to us,

for the amazing things that you've done

and the praise that you have rightly won.

I hope, *Dreimissa*, that these words
will do you justice.

Daring to do battle against far-superior odds,
you stripped the reputation of an invading army
and left them,
for all their high-tech weaponry and influential friends,
with nothing.

Dreimissa, you have come into your own in this war
and grown into a role no other has played before.

Seeing you from a distance, nimble and lithe,
the way you zig-zag across the night, vital and bright-eyed,
a far-off speck … and then suddenly you've arrived.

A graceful note to your engine's beat,
stirring up courage, you lift us out of our seats,
confident in your presence, you won't overheat.

Now, with a group of fighters waiting within,
and the enemy trembling,
knowing the danger you bring:
this is the dual part
for which you hold a place in our hearts.

Dreimissa, squat and shorn,
It's no shame that on your slender frame
a heavy load is borne.

Day or night, cabin pulled away, gun mounted;
even in the glare of the midday heat
you stand up and are counted.

Topless, you return,
painted with the dust that has spattered your sides:
believe me, *Dreimissa*, this is good reason for pride.
It is no mark against your name,
in fact, small as you are,

low to the ground, open to the sky,
you have captured fat-necked tanks,
and brought down big bellied bomber planes.

Dreimissa, big thanks are due.
Injured people, riddled with bulletholes,
gushing with blood, have been rescued by you
back to safety in the nick of time.

It is you, *Dreimissa*, compassionate and kind,
fearless and agile, who fills out these lines.

The BMP
by Al Khadra

(Boyevaya Mashina Pekhoty; 'infantry fighting vehicle' was the first mass-produced infantry fighting vehicle (IFV) of USSR.)

As I climbed into the reclaimed tank in Meydjek
under the cooling branches of the acacia tree,
I saw the B.M.P that would make the Moroccan women fret
and bring a smile to the face of Sahrawi oppressed
who only wish to be free.

I saw that armoured tank, in which our soldiers could ride,
which could fly them and their guns across the desert miles.
I knew that on the day of the attack,
it would breach the enemy lines,
and carry a brave army
that is generous and wise,
and can wield its weapons skilfully
against an occupier who sits on stolen land,
a land which has never been his country.

Pillagers! Know that this tank will be merciless to its enemies
and will blast to dust the invaders and all their machinery.

The Berm
by Al Khadra

The king built the Berm

staking his claim behind landmines and snares,

but the army evaded it

and together took back

what was already theirs.

The Army
by Al Khadra

Oh you invaders!
You, who seize the home,
which the owners never asked you to take,
know that colonisers have come since the days of Rome
seeking subordinates they never could make.
Ambitious kings have claimed our land as their own
and found a resistance too strong to break.
And now you say, sitting on your throne,
to the reflection in your crown's polished jade,
There's a small nation, internationally alone,
I think I'll move in and invade.

When we heard him, our army was well-prepared
and hurled themselves fearlessly at him,
The King of Rabat had roused their ire
and they went out to snatch then
his painted crown and his gilded chair
and the weapons his retreating army abandoned,

and they used them then to breach his Berms

behind which his army cowered while they attacked him.

They derided the tactics which he had prepared

and the support of Reagan who backed him,

Machines of destruction ruined beyond repair

his army fled like rats then.

Shoo, shoo, little rats, into your hole!

Your donkey king will never forget it

he'll no more say with that arrogance of soul,

here's a small nation; I'll go and get it.

These are the deeds that our army have done,

Oh Allah, protect this heroic army.

HEROES

'Most of my heroes don't appear on no stamps'
- Public Enemy, 'Fight the Power' (1989)

Mohammed Sidi Ibrahim Bassiri
by Bashir Ali

Western Sahara's first agitator for independence, he organised Harakat Tahrir in the 1960s – the Liberation Movement of Spanish Sahara. "Obviously inspired by contemporary Arab and African liberation movements, the Harakat Tahrir called for the dissolution of traditional social structures as a step toward building national consciousness." At a demonstration on June 17, 1970, in al-Zamlah Square in L'Ayoune, Spanish forces killed between two and twelve of the protestors on the spot. The Harakat Tahrir was quickly suppressed, and Bassiri was arrested, never to be seen again. "Some Western Saharan nationalists call this the Intifadah al-Zamlah, their first uprising."[1]

Oh Allah,

I ask you with the greatest of your names

with which you have raised the skies,

take your servant Mohammed,

embrace him in mercy –

that distinguished leader

Mohammed, son of Sidi Ibrahim.

At a time before we knew ourselves

he saw what had to be done.

He found a disparate people

divided into tribes,

silenced by harsh oppression

---

1. *Western Sahara: War, Nationalism, and Conflict Irresolution;* Stephen Zunes and Jacob Mundy, Syracuse University Press, 2010.

and still he managed to unite us.
We knew the Bedouin ways,
could make the harsh desert a home
that feeds, shades and sustains us,
but we did not know how to end the occupation.
He kindled a light in the darkness of those days,
and his vision made real in Al Zamlah square
stands today as a symbol,
an example of how we must be.
Mohammed Bassiri, a martyr for us all:
his name will last for generations,
accept him, Oh Almighty, in heavens everlasting!

Back when the invader insisted
that we were not fit to manage our affairs;
when they kept us illiterate
and ignorant of their learning,
to prove us always dependent
on their guidance and protection;

when they gagged any mouth
that dared to defy them,
Mohammed Bassiri showed us the way.
He uncovered the truth of the theft of our homeland,
reckless of his pains, caring only for his people.
And even as the Spanish bullets rained down on us,
even as they dragged him away
never again to be seen in this lifetime,
Mohammed Bassiri was all that can be
of manliness, understanding, generosity,
his was the vision that helped us to see.

Oh Allah,
I ask you with the greatest of your names
with which you have raised the skies,
take your servant Mohammed,
embrace him in mercy –
that distinguished leader
Mohammed, son of Sidi Ibrahim.

Aminatou Haidar
by Bashir Ali

Prominent and well-loved activist (the 'Saharawi Ghandi' as she is sometimes known) she was imprisoned three times by the Moroccan authorities for her parts in the 1st and 2nd intifada. Her release in 2005 sparked a massive display of support. In 2008 she received the Robert F. Kennedy prize for human rights.

If all women and men

had taken the road of Aminatou Haidar,

all they would have achieved,

the sum of their deeds

would not have reached even the top of her sandal.

She sacrificed everything in selfless love for her people:

gave up her money, her comfort, her family

for the cause of liberation.

Surely you've seen this?

The work of Aminatou.

Do not just rank her against other women,

show me a man who can match her!

Tell me if you can, of an example,

living or gone,

who has done what she has done.

I, for one, have never found any,

nor have I heard of anyone who knows

of someone to measure against

Aminatou.

Wa shahidtu bima alimtu[1]

And I bear witness to what I know.

---

1. 'And I bear witness to what I know': a standard phrase asserting the speaker's honest intentions within the limits of any human knowledge, i.e. 'I speak the truth as I understand it'.

A Gift for the Saharawi Soldier
by Nadgem Said

Oh fighter, you who daily do your *tov*,

circling the *Kaaba* of your homeland with a Kalashnikov,

the victory is clear, we know what your *rashesh*[1] can do,

finish this struggle, the people's hearts are with you.

The matter is in your hand

that Kalash can liberate the homeland,

from which they have barred you,

let them know that with the song of the *rashesh* they can't argue,

not with a fighter who daily does his *tov*[2]

circling the *Kaaba* of his homeland with his Kalashnikov.

---

1. Slang for rifle. Lit 'sprayer'.

2. The poet uses the word 'Tov' to mean 'moving around' or, perhaps from context, 'patrolling' but it is the same word as the Arabic, 'Tawaf': the act of circumambulating the Kaaba at Mecca

Soldier, be the engine of the people's salvation,
it's time to reclaim our foundations,
shoulder the solution with your weapons,
we will only move forward with our actions.
Let these words be a path for your glory,
and you lives a part of the martyr's story.

Oh fighter, believe in the goodness of the living God,
circling the *Kaaba* of your homeland with a Kalashnikov.

Resistance Today

'To be a Polisario means to be committed to the liberation of your country. It is only such a concept as national liberation for which one can expect such total identification from the people. You cannot get that kind of commitment to a party or ideology.'

Ali Habib Kentaoui, former RASD ambassador to India, 1987.

Activists
by Bashir Ali

After all we've been through:
our lives lost in combat,
our people disappeared with no word or trace,
after those wasted years in distant jails
after the beatings and cruelties
and well-practiced punishments;
if somebody now betrayed the cause
it must be because they were born that way.

May I be far from selling out my people,
my mother tongue, my homeland, my soul
and the whole that I am part of.
What could be enough to replace these things?
No matter the bounty I am given,
it will always be less than my nation and my friends.

Do you think I could sell my soul

and become an empty shell?

Bow my head at jackboot feet,

kiss my dignity into the dust,

belittled, insulted and crushed?

Cursed be the tale-tellers,

who spoke sugared words trying to turn me a traitor.

Resist
by Mahmoud Hadri

Resist your wounds; the desert is treeless:
a place of disaffection; peace and rest
can never dwell. Here our pain is ceaseless,
remains while we wear the chains of conquest.
L'Ayoune will drink no other drink but tears,
distilled inside that city's crystal eyes.
She's wrung with wrongs more than her back can bear;
oh brother, do not say ambition dies!

In desert waste we are the acacia trees,
the firm, unshaken valour which maintains
in times of danger, and difficulties
surmounts. Seek for stars and you'll reach mountains.
When we see L'Ayoune captive, the heart breaks,
but freedom survives the venom of snakes.

Intifada
by Hossein Mo'ulud

In Spring '05

the offensive of the second *intifada*

opened up the blooms of our struggle once more.

It was then, with reason on our side

and with steadfast unity;

propelled by all manner of sacrifices

(which can be made only by people

who know how just and right is their cause)

that the *intifada* blossomed again.

Informed by the lessons learned in the years of struggle,

strong with a determination finally

to reach the harvest time,

when we can at last gather the fruits of all this toil,

the strike on that great Saturday in May

was not hindered by the envious ones

who sit snidely in the wings.

Those blooms are truly empowering;

to cultivate them and to celebrate them

is the means of our liberation.

Anger of the People
by Mahmoud Hadri

Oh citadel of Glory!

Rise up today and come into our reach

we are weary of opinions and speech.

Drape anger now over every *haima*,

for the revolution of the people

is never empty of anger.

A poem for the Duty of the University Student Towards his Homeland
by Nadgem Said

University student, regaining homeland is an act of *abida*[1]
heed the call of your people and of your leaders.

Men of the university, use your pens,
there is no knowledge for knowledge sake
when your people ache
for exile to end.

Give voice to what you have learned:
describe the pains of your suffering race,
the abuse and agony that became commonplace
while the world's eyes were turned.

You cannot abandon your ancestors' ways.
As you advance with learning and books
remember the steps the martyrs took
to build the path to the present days.

---

1. Ritual duty / worship

You are wanted to put on victory's *dara*[2],
use your learning to remind us
that a homeland is something priceless
and help shake the dust of *intifada*.

University student, digitally connected, sophisticated readers,
the people are calling you as well as the leaders.

Isn't it enough this exile's history?
The invasion, exile and massacres,
because you have what the enemy fears in us:
the strain of victory.

Students, create the destiny of your people:
the moment is at hand,
bind together our divided land,
and let there be no sequel.

---

2. Traditional robes of Saharawi men

University student, regaining your homeland is an act of *abida*
hear the call of your people and the voice of your leaders.
Women of the university, we look to you too:
doctors and teachers, political leaders,
our women are renowned, it's true.

Your mothers built the camps while the men were away:
they brought up the children
and constructed the buildings,
now we need you to show us the way.

University student, regaining your homeland is an act of *abida*
heed the call of your people and of your leaders.

Students, use your knowledge to make a stand,
the cause of liberation is growing,
and the winds of victory are blowing,
rise up and go, live in the land.

Frente Polisario
by Beyibouh El-Haj

The Front took her seat among the nations that recognised her
and she was accepted,
in front of the grateful eyes of her well-wishers
and the bitter looks of the envious ones.

Perhaps all the envious need to do
is spread their envious chatter
and more envious will come running to their side.
But what have they ever done?
They did not build our homes, here, in exile,
and, worse still, they did give anything towards it.
They had better let the Front take her seat
among the nations that recognise her
in front of the grateful eyes of her well-wishers
and the bitter looks of the envious.

Of course, the envious were not there in the days of the
struggle.

They did not bring the women and children
to safety when the enemy's army were hounding them down.
They weren't there to offer the water of compassion
to the widows and orphans whose throats were dry with grief.
They cannot match the deeds of the martyrs
and cannot be measured against their size.
But when true men stepped into the breach
and took on the people's cares as dearly as their own,
and won for everyone a place, position and role;
then the envious shuffled uncertainly.
They were not sure whether to show hate or love
for The Front which had taken its place among
the nations that recognised her,
in front of the grateful eyes of the well-wishers
and before the bitter looks of the envious.

Take a look at our state, you envious ones,
see how well-structured and regulated,

how good natured she is,

how willing to overlook mistakes.

What she has done has been documented

and you have seen what principles she upholds.

You might think when you see the state

move one way then the other

that she doesn't know who helped

and who plotted against her;

but if you are not part of her

or have chosen another path,

at least let her be and leave her

in the place that Allah put her

when she won her seat

among the nations who recognised her.

Reflections

'It is as though they now live in separate ages of time, himself in the present and his spirit departing further into the past.'

Yvonne Vera, *Nehanda*, 1993

Advice
by Badi

Of the empty handed man who gives nothing
we cannot think ill,
but he who has, and will not give,
he carries a wrong with him still.

Landscape I
by Badi

Oh my eyes!
After the massacres and the exiled years,
return to look once more at the homeland.

See how the land lies:
bordered by Mount Grona and the hills of Darhd and Negai.
Look at the holy mountains of Norashin
and poor, neglected Mount Larwi.
Take it in, turn to the left and see!
Tinyir-ghat-Dawai.

Oh my eyes!
Look to the right,
see the sight of the Lamaileh mountains;
look and be healed.

Oh my eyes!
after the massacres and the exiled years,
return to look once more at the homeland.

Landscape II
by Badi

Oh my eyes!
After all that time absent from D'goush
and the mountains of Tingaphouf . . .
and after all that my soul has endured,
of long, never-satisfied longing . . .

Oh my feet!
after all this pain,
unable to walk in L'juad . . .
Know that to say these places'
names in praise,
brings them closer to the All-Merciful
Who watches over your pain:
my eyes, my feet and my soul.

And now, at last,
here is D'goush,
here is L'juad,
and here is Tingaphouf.

Tishuash
by Badi

(roughly 'nostalgia', but perhaps more correctly, 'the pleasure of remembering things that are past.')

All that has been has gone,

(how great the living and everlasting God!)

but how beautiful this scene is!

I see it sometimes –

no particular place –

just there with the goats,

like those nights I spent

at the mouth of a well,

making the wet sand my bed.

Enchanted by night's music:

the howl of wild dogs

and insects' whine.

Or in the watering season,

when the wheat is still to produce its seed,

I am there in the midst of the life of the camp,

doing some little thing about which you do not need to ask.

Or there we are
travelling in the dark before dawn,
from one stopping place to the next,
the only sound the swishing of camels' tails
before the sun has risen to our eye line;
walking on to those first lucid hours of the day
when the desert's features are clearest,
knowing both rocky valley
and the smooth.

And there again is the taste of tea,
flavoured with *da'i*,
in water sourced from the valley floor after the rains
or scooped from pools on concave rocks
where a river had run before;
when we were moving our camp from a dried-up well,
where the only firewood left was no better than kindling;
and I can smell that animal hide next to the spit
and see the clean bones beside that hide.

How come, my brother, you do not remember this;
the sweet life full of living?

It is no longer with us,
and if tishuash could bring it back
it would add tishuash
to the tishuash
of my tishuash.

To the Young People
Beyibouh El-Haj

Young people, listen,
I don't mean to be critical
but why do you turn your back on the homeland?
Young people, your generation is extraordinary,
you're progressive and sophisticated,
cultured and advanced.
Look at us: the old trees in their old places,
we know that the mountain ranges
will not pack up and leave the homeland,
so why should people abandon these places
when others have stayed and paid the price?
Could it be that you are afraid to die there?
So what?
The day the young people sparked the revolution
the youth were full of ambition.
They set their goals:
to live with dignity, and safety in our land;
renew that dream today
and the army will make it a reality.

Every day in the Occupied Zone,

the enemy wrings out the people

and squeezes them dry.

Go rescue them if,

by the time you finally get there,

there are any of us left.

Young people, listen,

I don't mean to be critical

but why do you turn your back on the homeland?

You, the new *Be'adan*[1],

born here in exile,

children of heroes

and heroes yourselves.

When the time comes

you will be unstoppable.

---

1. A respectful title bestowed on the 'true' Bedouin

The sound of clashing metal

makes you dance for joy;

you are a force that the enemy cannot restrain.

Yet now, you are wandering abroad

in foreign lands;

why are you so late returning home?

Are you waiting for that coward king

to suck dry the last of our resources?

This is not how we know

our young people to be.

Young people, listen,

I don't wish to be critical

but why are you turning away from the homeland?

I have spoken to those fighters from days gone by

and I have known them well:

those men who knew the K'lash

like a friend.

They felt its weight in their arms

and kept it with them.
When facing the enemy
they knew the only way is to advance:
this is the lesson from the people's army.

Oh young people!
You great intellectuals,
you need this example because
there is still a big test ahead of you.
Listen and take note of that lesson
for time will judge you
as good or as bad,
as right or as wrong.

Young people, be careful.
I don't mean to be critical
but are you turning your back on your homeland?

PART TWO

original poems by Sam Berkson

Arrival

At midnight in Tindouf airport
an un-uniformed un-official of an internationally
unrecognised government
hands us a form in Spanish, Arabic and misspelt English,
on which we record our entry into
R.A.S.D.
República Árabe Saharaui Democrática.

That night, a dog growled and barked and whined itself hoarse
at a waning full moon among the sandbrick houses,
grating its gravelly throat like a broken moped trying to start.
A choking complaint,
continually unanswered,
while the stars dance over the Sahara.

Mimi

Gracious host.
She watches us arrive
in the time of the flies
with our cases full of foreign foods and pills
and quickly learns our strange routines and requirements.

She cooks for twelve in the windowless kitchen
where the blue light of a gas stove dully illuminates
strings of drying goat which hang tenderising amidst the flies.
The slops are run off through a semi-circular cut
at the foot of the wall.

She holds herself on her haunches,
scraping and peeling and chopping
to make a dozen lunches,
she looks up,
raises an eyebrow, nods at my offer
and drags over a plastic stool.

Here is a peeler.

Here are some carrots.

Occasionally we point at things and say their names.

A big bowl of camel meat, rice or pasta

sucking the marrow off the bones.

I hesitate to help myself to more.

Eat it, she instructs,

I am not cooking for the goats.

Sweeping out the sand,

carrying in the water,

wringing out washing,

rolling a gas canister home,

keeping an eye on the

sons, daughters, nephews, nieces

who play around the compound,

picking up the pieces

when they all fall down.

There are bell-bright peals of laughter,
the knowing eyes that merrily watch me.
Qualified midwife,
now maker of home.

Work done for now,
you lie on side on a spread out carpet
under the darkening, star-sparkling night;
sprawling and tired,
crackling music on a battery radio.
Looking up again, you nod a *salaam*.
There is a cushion,
there is a carpet.
I recline to the sounds of spacious desert blues.

With the ten or so nouns we have to work with
we manage communication;
and you understand me somehow
in some uncommon language.

On the Arrival of UN Envoy, Christopher Ross, to Smara Refugee Camp, Tindouf.

The sun glares from the east-south-east
blazing through a thicket of flags.
Reds, blacks, whites and greens
hang loosely in the stillness.

A woman in a red *milfa*
steps foward, bends her black-scarfed head
over a T.V camera,
and pans it around the gathering crowd.

Busy officials direct us back, back, backwards,
clearing a path.

A semi-circle forms.

Voices rise, compete, collide in air space,
pick up, die down, surge and break,
each time gathering in volume.
Tongues holler ululations.

In front of us, along the newly formed parade ground,
khaki-clad men with battle-hardened faces
shake hands with each other.
Old men in pale-blue *daras* walk past
with gnarled limbs, hard sticks and gravitas.

Chants take up:

Men and women hand-in-hand
until we reach the motherland!

No compromise! No compromise!
All our country or we die!

Ross arrives.
Jeeps move in, army men surround,
women push forward,
push past, demand more space.
Ululations peak at screaming pitch.

Peace signs. Raised fists. Billowing flags.

Inside the District Centre,
Ross sits.
A white-haired, white man with a dark suit
and a modest-sized entourage.
He receives, in English,
the gracious delegations of the Christian-American
English-language centre;
and in angry Hassaniyah
the protestations of a headscarfed district governor.

Outside under the cover of an open *haima*,
facing the crowd,
he speaks, in Arabic,
to a TV camera and voice recorder.
The crowd of women, kept back a respectful distance,
persist in their chanting
despite some attempts to hush them.

Then, he is gone.

The army men thud bonnets,
move the crowd back, back.
The jeeps pull up, inch round,
slowly extricate themselves from the crowd
and drive off.

The refugees return to their forty-year-old
temporary shelters
to pray to Allah the Merciful,
to grant them a way which will bring them home.

Particulars

Prologue

For forty years
the people have waited,
fighting an opponent who will not retire,
while the one-eyed giants of the flesh-fed kingdoms
hold back the waves which could have swept clean the sands
when the sun finally set on the long day of empire.

How can you turn a blind eye to the particulars?

Green columns of figures
fluctuate senselessly on flickering screens.
In five fateful years
a billion dollars changed hands
as dance partners change and form new lines,
(see how round and round, they rotate -
360 dollars a minute)
and, in return, back from across the Atlantic came

packages of cluster bombs and heavy armoured cars;
Cobra helicopters fitted to spit their bitter venom,
hard-wearing tanks and airborne radar.

Picture the dockworkers who unloaded crates of artillery;
the boats that rode the ocean,
carrying supersonic jets to thunder over a nomadic enemy;
the men who laid ground sensor transducers
to snare the sandaled feet of goatherd guerrillas,
and who planted five million landmines
to decorate a defensive wall.

Fifteen hundred miles of wall.
The Great Berm of Morocco.
Behind which,
a great blank
in the conscience of the world.
How can you dim your sight with general trends and figures?
How can you turn a blind eye to the particulars?

I. Mahfoud

Imagine greybeard Mahfoud
in the strength of his youth
roaming for days away from his home
herding camels and goats
as all Sahrawi know,
back before shrapnel embedded in vertebrate bone
drained the sap from his trunk
so he can't stand on his own.
Now his brain flickers like a striplight
eyes that are hollowed by the horrors of the midnight,
buried alive in a twilight
where the fresh waters of life
mingle with the salt of oblivion,
waiting for vermilion judgment:
Let it fall in molten sulphur!

How vivid the nightmares.

Sleep is a memory, dim and afar,
like the peace of pavilion skies
thronging with the lights of a trillion stars.

II. Saeed

Saeed lies on his back
while his eyes trace the cracks in the ceiling,
most of his body cut off from all feeling,
across those stains on the tiles he has mapped out his opinion:

He says that
people without land are without value or worth,
his sacrifice on earth
a small price to pay for freedom.
He sees them, the youth,
and knows that from birth
they sucked a love of the land
with their mother's first
milk. They will never rest till
the blood of the martyrs is
washed by the rains
in a place where their ways
are never called strange:
their hills and their plains,
where they can walk in the tracks of their ancestors again.

But meanwhile, in exile:
keep this sight always
between the eyes,
take back the land
or like the others
we die.
And so he turns his face back to the ceiling.

III. Saleh

That the human spirit endures
is one of life's great mysteries.
Invisible to those whose arms command wars
and past the index of hardback histories,
we find you, Saleh.

Caught in the storm by accident of birth,
in the tempests of war
a bullet forked in white heat,
scorched your skull
and exploded in your eardrum.

Captured,

you stayed a decade

one of the world's long-forgotten,

lost to time in a Moroccan prison,

mocked by the cockroaches

who crawled under the door of your condition.

Be reasonable, they said,

and, between the beatings,

they offered money, a house,

just to beg for kingly pardon

and abandon the fight for your land.

But you and your comrades made your captors understand

that you would rather do the time than kiss the King's hand.

There are incentives stronger than reason and market forces,

and what the Human Will will do

should not really astonish us.

Now on the floor of your room

with a chess game set before us:

that perfect logic of an eastern game that the West

redressed in their image,

where white has first move and bishops scythe the diagonals,

I fear this old man learned lessons not found in the manuals.

You mutter and point, mumbling

cunning calculations

and seem to set me up for a humbling.

But your brain still shorts from that thunderstorm,

occasional white-outs cause your mind to wipe out

and confuse your concentration.

I claw out a victory

and take leave of your easy hospitality

departing with laughter,

a handshake and that famous generosity

IV. Bashiri

Move next door to Bashiri,

who at sixteen years young,

patience strung

tight on the rigid frame of his father's rule,

left all that he knew

to find work in L'Ayoun.

Determined, unschooled,

he beat his heels down the long road to the colonial capital
where the Atlantic crashes against Spanish *edificios*.
Another juvenile with a restless mind,
he found that job that all young men find
who seek release for the youthful riot
without the wherewithal to buy it.
Didn't know his age hardly,
signed an X on the dotted line
of Franco's colonial army.

He had known nothing of states and the stakes of the game,
But his spirit soared at the whispered call of *jihad*
against the infidel he served.
Months went by and he earned a little trust,
directed a Land Rover truck
to drive straight into a Polisario trap;
delivered seven Spanish hostages, their weapons and their car.
The men they gave back, but Bashiri found a new kind of war,
fighting Moroccan muslims
seeking to run up their flag
on the poles Europeans had left them.
A guerilla army, where the leaders shared food and hardship
with the people who followed them,

no stars on the arm, no servants nor castes,

he learned the art of the raid and the fight for freedom.

A brigade of five young recruits,

only one Kalashnikov between them.

You should have seen him!

So smart in uniform,

a woman who'd agreed to marry him

and then the very next day,

he was behind the wheel in a Land Rover raid

that got too close to a mortar's range

and the rest, as they say, is history.

It was all going well when I strapped myself into that carrier.

I should have known that woman would bring bad luck,

I should never have agreed to marry her.

The room explodes with laughter.

Now his hand holds mine,

his fingers curl where the muscles

no longer receive the impulse to straighten them.

Al-Jazeera on the satellite,

we debate democracy and the state of things

Bashiri, bed-bound:

we listen and laugh along

as he recounts the lessons learnt from those years,

and our eyes glint with tears.

Epilogue

These are some of the Western Saharans
who had to flee their land.
They fought to hold off a Moroccan monarch
who wanted a royal parade ground to march his colours in,
a war to divert those who were eyeing too closely his position.
Phosphate mines and fishing rights a little compensation
for that billionaire King,
whose friends loaned arms, wrote blank cheques
to maintain the alliance; interwove their general conditions,
as they underwrote his moves,
in a game of abstract *realpolitik*.

Now on this island in the desert's billowing waves,
the wind blows hot among the blocks of the hospital
for the paralysed, the brain-damaged, the limbless.
Sand squints our eyes and scratches our nostrils.
We meet the marooned sailors
whom no Odysseus came to save,
and who regularly wish peace upon us.
Tongues click, heads nod, glasses of tea clatter on a metal tray,
and I try to learn a little more of the particulars.

Friday Afternoon in Smara

The heat burns everything still.
The wind that fills silk curtains does not stir us.
The goats that hobble or hurry outside our window
do not convince us with their reality.
Flies are nothing but the whine of a broken clock
that has, for however many lost hours, patently stopped.
Time as unmoving as the rusting car that sits
with its axles resting on bricks.
Neighbours have returned to sleeping houses,
the tea things in their metallic silence,
the stove unlit, the dishes packed away
and the water hose warming on the washing line.

Only the children ignore the signs.
They whisper among us, knowing we are dead,
picking seriously at the scabs on their knees and arms,
restless with the budding energy of young lives
in a desert of hopes and heat-blasted time.

Sketch:
Women's Centre, Smara

In the patterned yellow *milfa*
she sits with warning eye,
and turns to the watching world a lethargic disdain.
She shoots disinterested sideways glances;
clicks her tongue in hard-won approval.

Nighttime

Soap suds slosh into sandy yard.

Shit moves mockingly round the open end of a blocked pipe.

Remnants of distant stars hint at infinity.

Morocco still occupies the homeland.

Landscape

The sand of the Maghreb Sahara
is blown and shifted across
thousands of miles of landscape.
Myriad variations of arid:
from the south-west,
where Richat's *eye of the desert* stares
out of a forty kilometre-wide iris,
so perfectly round it was once thought to be
the site of an asteroid landing;
north and east to the swelling Erg Chebbi dunes
where rheumatics come in the hottest part of the summer
to bake neck deep in the orange sand
and free up their stiffened joints;
and south again to the Al-Haggar mountains,
three thousand metres up
to the fortress-hermitage of Charles de Foucauld:
an ascetic French aristocrat
with a calling for loneliness and holy missionary,
who sent up his prayers from

the basalt organ pipes of solidified lava;
before he was hunted down and murdered
by bandits unsympathetic to his beatitude.

Across the desert's western regions,
the nomadic Rgaybat, Dalim, Tiknah
and other Hassaniyah speaking people
followed for centuries the green routes of the rains,
struck camp at oases;
annually took camels on month-long journeys
to trade for the goods of settled cities;
fought occasional wars;
sung elegiac or squabbling poetry;
followed their version of Islam
disseminated from early Arab conquerors,
a religion that took root slowly
while empires rose, clashed and fell.

Towards the end of what we call the fifteenth century,
the uncouth Christian tribes
north of the narrow stretch of the Mediterranean
had begun to coalesce into nations
and were developing a taste for gold, spices and slaves.

These they would trade to pay for their pleasures:
buy land, build palaces, boost status.
Tri-masted ships, carved out of Europe's decimated forests,
lateen-sailed to beat against the winds,
skirted the wide boundaries of the unpassable Great Desert
and slid their shallow keels up fertile river basins,
teeming with gold seems and commodifiable heathens,
Seeking out people to buy and to sell.
The barren Sahara was no more than a barrier to bypass,
but along the way,
the hot Atlantic coast saw its cities occasionally raided.

As cheap free labour became less expensive
than the enslaved version,
and as revolutions and war shook Europe and its colonies,
the trade in humans came to an end.
The mysteries of the billowing desert now began to attract
adventurers.
Rumours of Timbuktu, city of gold,
mystical source of the glittering river Niger,
fed a fad for discovery.
And it was not long before
thick smoke billowed from the great library of Smara,

and garrisons grew on the rocky cliffs of ocean harbours.
New sheikhs and sultans greedily accepted
the assistance of pale skinned conquerers;
and, trailed with European gunpowder,
they laid paths for colonial powers
to find new kingdoms to parade in,
new markets to trade in,
new products to claim as their own.

Berlin 1884.
Epauletted men recline in mahogany chairs,
smoke bright-leaf Virginia tobacco
over silk-embroidered damask tablecloths
and rule straight lines across maps of Africa.
New territories are baptised and new names recorded.
Spain christens its pistol-shaped pieces
of the western reaches of the desert;
Río de Oro its grip, the barrel Saguia el-Hamra:
Spanish Sahara.
Falling along the tumbling Atlantic coast
south of the Dra'a river,
stopping at the straight lines of its eastward border,
its right angles score the limits of the Francophone colonies:

Morocco, Algeria, French West Africa.

For twenty years the European agreement survived,
each Berlin Conference guest free to feast
on the shared-out portions of the continent.
Free, that is, until they blew that *entente cordiale* to pieces
in the trenches of Belgium and France
and drowned it in the straits of Gallipoli.
And, as if the illimitable forces of cause and effect,
the unjust deserts served up to societies
whose masters dine on the finest flesh
and who sip wine that runs blood-red,
were not satisfied with the extent of destruction,
the children of the millions dead and of the survivors
were sent out to die again twenty years later
in another terrible ruckus for power.
On the ashes of London, Dresden, Hiroshima,
among the skeletal mountains piled high in Poland,
claims of supremacy lay tattered,
bankrupt world powers lost their grip on their colonies,
and new ideas of independence
flourished in Africa.
But deep in the Sahara,

the whirlwinds of world war had blown elsewhere
and left the colony largely unscathed.
It was the post-war hurricanes of France and Spain,
the localised repression and unprecedented drought
which settled the cities in Spanish Sahara.
Resistance grew there.
In L'Ayoune, the twenty-five year old capital,
Al-Zamlah square ran with blood
as protestors pressed for freedom
in a storm of Spanish bullets.

Al-Khanga, 1973.
Above the black scree of stony desert
a small band of men, faces turbaned
to protect them from the wind-whipped sand,
the scouts of a troop of rebels,
survey the defences of an isolated garrison.
Spotted, surprised, out-numbered, out-equipped
they are duly arrested by *Tropas Nomadas*
in the name of Generalissimo Francisco Franco.
Who is this Franco, brother?
asks one of the rebels,
calm through the bars of his cell.

His unused rifle rests against crumbling plaster
on the wall behind the Saharawi soldiers
who have arrested him.
They sit on plastic chairs
and consider his words thoughtfully.
Why are you turning your back on your people?
the prisoner asks them.
Inside the cell,
flies rub their hands over a plate of untouched biscuits.

When the rest of the band launch the attack
to liberate their captured comrades,
are they surprised to find the Spanish-paid soldiers
surrender quite peacefully
and sign up to the movement
which declares itself from that garrison,
Frente Popular para la Liberación
de Saguia el-Hamra y Río de Oro
the region's popular front?
The Polisario.
Within two years

change was as inevitable as its outcome uncertain.
U.N resolutions upheld self-determination,
Polisario supporters prove resolutely determined.
Across the Moroccan border
but King Hassan was drumming up disturbance.

Madrid, 1975.
Through the late Baroque
pillars of Palacio de La Moncloa
fifteen years since Franco
declared that the Spanish flag
would fly forever in its Saharan province,
grave ministers assemble
to greet their ageing *caudillo*.
Generalissimo, 350,000 Moroccans
will march on Spanish Sahara by the end of next week.
His face is gaunt now, eyes half-closed,
a sag of jowl hangs where infirm age has deflated
that balloon of fleshy face.
His chair seems, for the first time, to dwarf him.
His minister continues,

The fools consider themselves mujahidin

on holy jihad *to rid their territory of the infidel.*
Of course, the truth of the matter...
Jefe?
He groans, slips and slides.
His doctor rushes to his side.
He will cling to what remains of life
through a month of heart attacks and coma.
Western Sahara's weaponless assassination.

The centre cannot hold.
Keen to take the reins of power,
in Layoune, Juan Carlos on horseback
inspects his colonial regiments,
still straight backed and saluting,
though depleted by desertions.
Now, more than half the seats of the *Jama'a* assembly
are empty.
Desertion fever has infected them too.
The debates of Spanish Sahara's puppet government
have a hollow ring to them.
The clamour of protest is louder outside.
In Rabat,

military commanders pace the shaded colonnades

of the Moroccan palace,

respectfully urging their king to action.

Across the Atlantic, voices are raised in the Oval Office.

I think the UN should take on more of these problems.

God damn, we shouldn't have to do it all and get a bloody nose.

That was President Ford.

The Sahara is a mess.

When Kissinger the others listen.

If he – (King Hassan) *– doesn't get it,*

he is finished.

The hope is for a rigged UN vote, but if it doesn't happen...

Behind closed doors of international diplomacy,

the re-instated Spanish monarch and the Mauritanian president

meet with Hassan.

So far Allah has protected him

from coup, revolution and assassination.

A deal is cut.

Spain will keep the fish,

if Morocco can have the land.

The sky they leave to God

and his satellites.

From the south come the Mauritanian army.
From the north, the Moroccans.
The Green March makes its symbolic way to the border.
People chant, carrying their flags,
declare their obedience to the dream of Greater Morocco,
their King and their God.
Then they are shuttled back again.

Meanwhile: planes, tanks, infantry.
The land is rocked by mortar shells and bombs.
People flee. Gather what they can and leave.
On foot, on camel, in car. Heading east
away from the carnage in their homeland.
For the Polisario fighters days and nights blur as one.
Awake for hours. Little food. Rest impossible.
Constant messages: Land Rovers, field phones.
seeking to secure safe passage
for a hundred thousand Saharawi.

And bombs. Always bombs.
Houses slammed. Families gunned down,

bodies dumped in mass graves that the shifting sand
will gradually reveal after fifteen years of war.

Even in the chaos of conflicts, all things find their pattern.
Mauritania defeated, they retract their claim
and agree to respect the border.
Grand powers send more and better weapons for Hassan's army.
But guerrilla raids in this hot and barren landscape
are sapping the morale of the Moroccans,
chasing an elusive enemy
who can slip quietly to safety
across the porous Algerian border.

Wait for them to come to you.
Make the borders of your province.
Build up your defences.
We'll give you ground sensors, satellites, radar, artillery.
let them figure out a way to get behind you.

Steadily Morocco build berms to hold their position.
Once a section is completed, another must be built,
each time further eastward,
until the line of occupation is finally marked.

A raised sand bank stretches 2700 kilometres,
leaving the Polisario a handful of arid settlements
and barren sand dunes along the Mauritanian border.
The Berm: tangled with barbed wire,
marked by fences and trenches,
watched over by 170,000 Moroccan soldiers
and punctuated with the waiting springs
of seven million landmines.

Twenty-five years of uneasy ceasefire.
An ambassador writes,
the U.S. wished things to turn out as they did,
and weapons and advice still flow across the Atlantic.

Now in less than temporary refugee towns
near the isolated city of Tindouf,
South Western Algeria,
the wind whips up the sand into an angry storm.
It covers tents and goat pens and food aid trucks,
satellite dishes, solar panel and camel dung;
it stings eyes and clogs up lungs.

Smudges of hovering sandcloud block out the sun,

guy ropes flap madly in the gale,

the refugees must fix what they can and wait for it to end,

wanderers, now settled,

the exiled República Árabe Saharaui Democrática

Tea with Beyibouh

'bitter like life, sweet like love, soft like death'
the traditional order of the three cups of tea customarily served to guests

The billows pump the coal.

Frankincense floats lightly

through the four-doored tent,

open at all sides to chance breezes or wandering strangers.

Squares of light across the carpeted floor

hint at that glasstop glare

of the engulfing desert

that swallows vast swathes of the continent.

But, here, enclosed in cooling gloom,

we are pitched on the edge of the settlement,

where sandbricked camp meets expanding Sahara,

and goats and camels pick about the rubble on the frontier,

penned hundreds of miles from

the land the poets used to sing of,

the other side of a wall and landmines and diplomatic impasse.

The flies flicker and fuss busily.

Tea is poured and repoured from cup to cup.

The ceremonial liquid, strong and dark.

Glasses clatter on metal tray.
Bitter like life.

The tea is the generosity of
Beyibouh El-Haj,
fourth generation poet,
but once a camel herder in Spanish Sahara
like the rest of them.
He was nearly fifty when the Moroccans came,
moved out in the night when the soldiers stormed their homes.
They escaped east to exile carrying little more than
a head full of memories.

Eighty if he's a day.
He talks with a vigour
and energy that stirs the room to life,
apparently undimmed by the years.
People watch him.
His wife, working the billows,
watches him;
casts a look that is proud
but mindful he does not overstretch himself.
His grandson shyly shuffles in,

then clamours for attention.
He sprawls in his lap,
pulls on his ears,
watches him
flashing two rows of milkwhite milkteeth
and unconcealed affection
until he leaves at his grandfather's orders.

We sweep up the tea cups, pass them back
and, for the second time, his wife pours the brown liquid
from cup to cup in sweeping arcs,
heading each glass with a froth to sift the sand and dust,
enriched with sugar,
freshened with mint.
Sweet like love.

He has the gift of laughter.
He speaks in slow, guttural Hassaniya,
considers and weighs his phrases,
winds up towards the breathy punchline
that breaks us all out in laughter.
He slaps hands with everyone.
And another tea is poured.

His poems stripped King Hassan's rhetoric
and mocked his naked intentions.
They breached the berm,
they roared through skies,
no S.A.M could touch them.
Now in time of theoretical ceasefire
when demonstrations are besieged and battered and broken
behind global media silence;
after decades of underweight and undernourishing food aid;
at a time when civilian settlers are rearranging borders;
after remaining as exiles unmoving through the years
while U.N workers serve their time and envoys come and go;
his poems bring laughter, keep memory alive,
enliven our tea talk,
way past the third step in this familiar ritual.
Tea drained to the dregs,
just a taste on the tongue when there's nothing left.
Soft like death

Is there crime on the camps?

I ask.

The young, he says,

they want things straight away.

They don't want to wait for them.

And so, some, some steal and thieve.

And, yes, he says,

many have been abroad and seen on TV

images and places that shift the borders of wants and needs.

But they are young, he says,

and this is how young people have always been.

Girls on Tour

(Olive Branch Youth Theatre on Tour; L'Ayoune - Smara refugee camp, Tindouf; 2013)

The sky burns red, fades to pinks
to greys, to white.
Behind us, the *waleia* mosaics with square mudbrick houses
quarried from the sand of the desert
that gave these people their name.

A century of unwanted interference,
decades of war and struggle
have wound up here.
Tessellating near identical square compounds,
scored with sandy paths
and dotted with dusty blue tents
in an overlooked corner
of Algerian Sahara.

Beyond the bounds of that settlement
of less than temporary homes
the dust rolls across the desert's majestic miles.
Here an underground stream

supports a line of low-lying dusty greens,

there, a scree of charred black rocks

disturbs the uniformity of the landscape.

It is a billowing ocean of sand.

And from a passing plane

we are two black boxes tacking across its vastness,

spewing up a thin spray of sand.

Move closer and you would see two Toyota Land Cruisers.

They each carry fifteen or so members of

a newly formed all-girl youth theatre

on tour between the refugee camps,

an hour's drive apart.

Leaning out of the windows into the desert wind,

the girls holler, scream happily,

ululate excitedly, wave RASD flags,

flash two-fingered peace signs

across the shimmering glare

of the Sahara.

Why you should never do translation in the house of your Saharawi translator.

For why?

Look: because first, his mother will make you lunch,

and it will be a great lunch,

honouring the guest who has come from a country far away

to be with the family on this special day.

And although the government of that country

has consistently blocked

the Saharawi right for self-determination,

it is important not to show ill-will to the people of that nation,

and to show that Saharawi welcome guests

from wherever they come.

And, in any case, there are many other people here to eat today.

So many, in fact, that children will have to bring the food

on two large round dishes just to fit it all in,

and there will be two cross-legged circles

on the carpeted floor of the room,

which is your translator's bedroom and his tailoring workshop

and also the family living and dining room.

And after the apples and the yoghurt
and after your translator has cleared it all away
and all the guests have poured the plastic kettle of water
for their fellow guests to clean their chicken-greased fingers
and some of the guests have prayed
their afternoon prayers as conscience has dictated,
and we have all started to recline again
on the room's hard cushions,
then you can start on the translation.

But not before tea is made.

And your translator, being the host of this occasion,
must make the tea.
And to produce a glass cup of tea for all the guests
there must be endless boiling of water
and sugar and tea leaves and herbs
in a small kettle on the brazier's coals
and the pouring of tea from glass to glass
and the pouring of tea back into the kettle
and the pouring of more water into the kettle
and the pouring of tea back into the glass,
so that, before the first cup of tea is ready,
there must be at least forty minutes of preparation.

Then, having drunk the tea
(which takes about ten seconds)
and returned the glasses back to the translator,
you are ready for the translation.

But now there is a whole committee of interpreters.

And the committee can dispute such questions as may arise,
such as, in the second half of the first line,
where the poet uses a phrase which,
being no longer in current language,
is a troublesome point of interpretation,
so that we cannot be certain of its meaning,
until two members of the committee have spoken on the phone
to a friend or relative who can be sure to know such things.
And, although the poet in question lives only a short walk away
along the sandy rows between the sandbricked houses,
to go ask him in person, as you suggest,
would oblige him to receive you as guests
and to make tea and to welcome you
and that would be too much,
especially, as here, your translator hasn't even made
the second cup of tea.

So your translator begins again to prepare the tea,
interrupting the task only to read out the disputed text
so that the phrase can be relayed on either of the two phone calls
to the wise people at the other end of the lines.
And after an hour or so has passed, you can move onto line two.
And some of the committee have left now
so things should flow more smoothly.

But first there are new guests for everyone to greet.

And, like a wind-up toy of ritualistic and joyful greetings
everyone in the room is exchanging *salaams* and how-are-yous
and slapping handshakes
until they all wind down to a stop
and we are all sure that everyone is welcome
and everyone is fine
and we can explain to the new guests what we are doing,
and ask their opinion on the difficult phrase in line one.
And soon your translator's phone will ring
and he will exchange greetings with whoever is calling
and discuss whatever has to be discussed
and then we can return again to the problem of the poem.

Which is now going on to mention sadly –
or perhaps with intense longing
in a way that reflects the process of memorisation –
some places in the occupied land of Western Sahara
that no one too young to remember 1975 will know
due to the harsh and oppressive occupation by Morocco.
So it is hard at this point to know if one place in the poem
is a mountain, as most of the committee think,
or whether it is a valley,
or a small hill as someone else is insisting,
but it's okay because your translator can ask his father
when he returns from his tailoring shop in the market.
And talking of family, now your translator is needed
to perform some duties for his mother
so we must wait for his return while the flies buzz busily about
and the sun throws its squares of light on the carpeted floor.
And now your translator returns and you can get on again with
the translation –
after the third cup of tea is ready.

And so it goes on through more guests and more *salaams*
and more tea and more discussion, depatures and phone calls
and more hand slapping and jokes and good-natured debate

and the arrival of your translator's father

(who is fairly convinced that it is, after all, a mountain)

and though you find yourself moving more and more out

towards one of the low square windows cut into the wall

to watch the goat pen and the eternal boy with the stick and tyre,

while the discussions continue without you,

by the time you have finished, six hours after you started,

you will feel great friendship with everyone

and you will read out to what is left of the assembled committee

the first rough sketch of the first ever English translation

of one of the great Badi's fifty years' worth of poems.

And there is much hand slapping

and a real sense of collective achievement.

And now, as the first stars are appearing above the camel pen,

in the crescent-moon-lit, opal blue desert sky,

you have only eight more recordings of Hassaniyah poems

to transcribe into Arabic and then translate into English

before you leave for the airport tomorrow evening.

Sketch:
Morning, Smara

Two men in military fatigues

walk hand-in-hand slowly

through the desert wasteland by the checkpoint

at the edge of the camp,

discussing something thoughtfully.

One bald head, one grey;

as the hot desert sun rises inexorably

through the dust cloud

that hangs over the morning.

Bendir

I. Some of them have faces that tell you they were in the army:
hard, weather-beaten, a little bored,
and when you see them drive
you know for sure.
Tailing a car impatiently
around a long blind corner,
they'll hammer down the throttle as soon as
they can safely sight a space to pass.

And when your driver pulls off onto the unmarked desert tracks
you can doubt no more.

Needle hovering at 80k,
he thunders over the rutted tracks
of this sparse unsignposted landscape,
spewing a wake of dust as we chew a path through the vastness.
From one hundred yards he can size up a line in the land
that might be firm rocky scarp,
treacherous soft sand

or half-hidden trench
and he knows instinctively
for which he slows down.

He knows it,
just as his grandparents
must have known where to dig a well
or to find shade for their camels;
just as I, cycling in London,
can read which red light to trespass,
or prophesise, as I career down the centre line,
where the gap in the traffic will arrive
to let me back inside.

Surely he must have done this before
in circumstances that would test him more
hurtling with nerves steeled firm
at an armed Moroccan base along the berm.

II.
Some days later I get to speak to him –
the man appointed to drive me
to the little military airport

where my journey home begins.

Bendir,
who speaks much better English than he previously let on,
now, in his self-taught fourth tongue,
spliced with French,
accented with dramatic hand gestures,
tells me some of his story.

After the ceasefire, it seems,
the Polisario reabsorbed a number of its soldiers
as drivers for the government.
'My chef,' he says, 'told me:
"Here you are until the next order."
That was 1991.
I am still waiting for the next order.'
Chopping hands enforce the point,
mobile phone ringing as he negotiates the darkening,
desert road towards the edge of the camp.
'Now when visitor comes I drive them,
very safe.'

At the sand-bagged checkpoints on the edge of the Polisario's state-in-exile,

Bendir jokes with the Saharawi soldiers on night-duty

and fifty yards on,

obligingly produces papers for

the sullen looking Algerians who patrol our re-entry

into the host nation's territory.

'Between us and the Algerian militaire', he explains,

'There is big difference.

A militaire here,'

he indicates the tall, muscular solider disappearing behind us,

'He works to take money home for his family.

When the end of the month arrives,

he sees his son, his daughter, his woman,

his home.'

I remember the Air Algiers man at the check-in desk

who told me he had fled his country

rather than do a tour of duty,

here in Tindouf,

the arse end of desert nowhere.

'And the Moroccan army?' I ask.

'There is no comparison!' and a flat palm thuds the edge
of the steering wheel in emphasis.
He swerves past a battered family Ford
as dark descends from the desert foothills.
'A Morocco militaire,
he does not need to die!
He does not need to be captured.
He does not need to be invalid.
We want that.'
The moon is rising full and bright in the evening sky.
'A Saharawi solider does not care
if he dies today or tomorrow.
The Moroccan is fighting, he is fighting,
but a Saharawi is fighting
to bring his family home.
And where is my home?' Bendir asks me.
My home is not here.
My home is Western Sahara:
the home of my wife, and my father,
my brother, my sister, my cousin.
None of them are home.
I am fighting to go home.
That is the difference.'

Bendir cranks the truck back into fifth gear.

One time, he tells me,

one comrade in his company

refused take part in a raid on Moroccan held Dhakla.

They remonstrated with him.

He had been engaged to a woman in the city before the war,

when her family had called it off.

'I am liberating Western Sahara,'

the spurned lover had insisted,

'but I'm not liberating Dhakla!'

We laugh together at his story.

'And the Polisario tactics,' I ask, 'they are different too?'

'The Polisario army is *mobile*,' (he says it in the French way)

We can be here at eight o' clock

and there at twelve o' clock',

arms flying off the wheel

and jabbing into the night,

'We do not hide behind a Berm waiting,

you compris?'

The Moroccan soldier does not know where we will be.

And they know they are making very bad things in Western

Sahara,

and he is afraid if Polisario capture him,

one day…'

An explosion of both arms .

'See?'

years of waiting and suffering and strained patience,

executed in sharp, efficient blows.

'The Polisario is very forgiving.

We do not treat our prisoners with torture,

we do not kill civilians,

we do not use terrorism,

but the Moroccan militaire knows

that they are making torture in Western Sahara

and they are very afraid.'

Bendir trained in the Algerian airforce as a pilot,

hoping one day to reconquer his homeland

from the tumult in a cloudless sky,

but when he joined the Polisario's war

there were no still no planes for him to fly.

So, for a time he drove lorries all over the Sahel,

from Spain to Mauritania,

until he had retrained as a tank driver.

'My company, we know how to get behind the Berm.

So at night time we drive to the wall,

sometimes we have infra-red but it not always work

so I drive without it.

I think is better.

But we get to the Berm

dig up the landmines

and then we dig them back on Moroccan side.

The next day: Lorries, tanks, trucks…

BOOM!

All gone.'

Hoist by their own petard.

'We find stores of weapons, of machine guns

but we cannot touch because then they know we are there.'

In a passing layby, miles from anywhere, a parked car.

Bendir explains how Algerian couples come out here from

Tindouf to drink illicit alcohol and snatch illicit kisses,

having to pay off the police if they catch them there.

'In Western Sahara army the chef is not a superiority,'

he continues,

'He has more responsibility, different role,

but you and he, you have the same job.

We have the same *objectif*.

It is the same with the president.

I can meet with Mohamed Abdelaziz

and I can come and salute with his hand,

"You are president, and I respect you,

but president of what?"'

His hands wave towards the roar of the wind that passes us.

'Sahara is not free. Sahara is under Moroccan control.

If Western Sahara is free,

then, after that, ok, if you need to be a king,

then we discuss.

But important now is *objectif*.'

As the airport approaches,

he takes the Land Cruiser into its security chicanes.

Though the tank he once drove now rusts in a shed unused

Bendir is still a Polisario man.

'In twenty years,

this is my third car.

In 6 month, sometimes, not obligated, I have 100 euro
but I have everything guaranteed:
food, rice, oil, basic things.
Also to be hospital.
If the hospital is not able to cure you
they send you or family outside.'

Mission accomplished,
he parks the British poet by the entrance
to the tiled floor departure lounge.

'Some Saharawis after the ceasefire they work like a business,
you compris?
They have a job, they are not working for the government.
You cannot treat this one as me.
I work voluntarily. I have my hundred euros
for my six months, yes,
but sometimes it is six months, sometimes seven months.
Sometimes they tell you, maybe, this time there is not 100, have
eighty euros,
it is not obligated.'

III.

We shake hands, hug and depart.

At the airport,

bored Algerian soldiers watch the football listlessly.

People fill in forms, drink coffee from plastic cups.

Suits and headscarves, sweat and luggage,

pushing in gendered queues to be first in the next waiting room.

A singing group of Saharawi women

cause consternation by the metal detectors at the entrance.

I settle into the passivity of modern travel,

(how many months to Algiers by camel?),

present my passport to customs,

put my hand-luggage through security.

I sit and wait to take a plane back home

with Bendir's words still with me.

Biographies

Al Khadra Mabrook

b. Tiris, circa 1938

One of the best known Saharawi poets internationally, partly because of the fame of her granddaughter, singer Aziza Brahim, Al Khadra's nickname, 'poet of the rifle' is a reflection of years of poetry that she says 'has always been for the revolution'.

The first time I met her (in the 'sickness season'), she had just come back from hospital after a bout of illness and we sat in a tent covered with flies while she patiently answered questions and posed for photographs.

She says she doesn't remember much of her 'rambunctious' childhood, other than she and her family lived the simple life of the Bedouin, on the move to find water and greenery. As a young woman who could not read or write, she learned poetry and songs (the distinction between them was slight) by listening to them and attending moonlight recitals. In the pre-war period, she would chant poems that mainly 'celebrated female beauty' but after the war, 'there was only one focus: to inspire and to encourage, to praise an army which rescued people who were in danger, at great risk to themselves'. Unlike the more celebrated Mauritanian poets and singers, whose language and culture has much in common with their Northern neighbours, she emphasises that the Saharawi poets are not singing for a living but composing their poetry for a cause and to celebrate heroism.

First meeting her, an old woman, looking a little frail and worn out from her illness I was struck firstly by the power of her voice and then by the revolutionary content of her poems. She is a tall women, obviously robust despite the ill-health, direct in her poems and in her conversation, with a voice that could fill stadiums. She spoke those poems looking directly at me, knowing that I would not understand the language but willing me to feel the sense in the words. More than any of the other poets I met, she delivered her words with a lively drama and well-developed sense of performance. On both occasions she wanted to hear one of my poems and despite her condition, was gracious and hospitable. Apologising for the inadequacy of the gesture, I gave her money as I did all the poets whose work I have translated. She brushed my apology aside, 'You are the only person who comes here who has given me anything.'

As we left her tent, she took aside Mohamed and myself, told him of the responsibility of the youth and warned me of the danger of opposing Morocco. 'You are brave,' she told me over-generously, 'I know you will meet an enemy face-to-face but you must beware of an enemy who will stab you in the back.'

Mohamed Mustafa Mohamed Salem
'Badi'
b. Western Sahara, 1936

Now in his 70s, Badi is a much revered poet among Saharawi. Born under Spanish occupation, Badi was a goat and camel herder until 1960 when his family lost most of their herd in a severe drought, and with it their livelihood. Forced to find a way to earn a living, he enrolled in the Tropas Nómadas of Franco's colonial army. They escaped their homeland after the Moroccan invasion.

I met Badi just before sunset in his tent in Smara camp, where many of his family were sitting too, including his granddaughter who is studying Hassaniyyah poetry at university in Algeria. There were goats and children playing outside. For some reason I remember a cat, but perhaps I've made that up. A small man with glasses, Badi proved generous, interesting and lively company despite health problems affecting his lungs and eyes – a common condition on the camps, which are hit by frequent sandstorms.

He started by telling me about the history and form of

Saharawi poetry. Before the war, he explained, all poetry was accompanied by music and performed with a singer, but it is still now considered to be an art form very close to song, with strict rhythm and rhyme patterns.

After a time, he grew bored of lecturing me and asked me about the history of English poetry. I did my best to explain what I knew and we debated whether free verse could be poetry. Badi thinks not. He recited for me a couple of short and profound poems, and then again turned the tables on his interviewer, and asked me to read him one of mine. I read him 'Ode to the Bicycle' from my first collection, prefacing it with the explanation that it is a poem for people who prefer simpler, cleaner forms of technology to the faster and more polluting methods of transport. His eyes lit up when this sentence was translated.

'Poets have always liked the simple life!' he told me.

After hearing this, he gave me 'Tishuash'. Mohamed, Chaka and I finally came round to translating this poem on the last night of my stay and late into the desert night I could see what a strikingly profound poem it is for Saharawi refugees. It retells the nomad's desert knowledge and recreates with a melancholic beauty the traditional life of herdsmen which many Saharawi have never known. It is replete with words which even my local translators had to ask about; words like 'srei' meaning 'the travelling done before dawn' or 'torda', which is 'a small hole dug where water lies close to the surface after the rains in the middle of a valley'. These words of an oral language, this intimate understanding of the desert have almost been forgotten after forty years of forced settlement and thus their recital in poetry is itself an act of resistance. They are the Inuit's apocryphal 'hundred words for snow' and an interesting challenge to translate. However, as is clear in the words of 'Landscape II', the act of remembering these lost places and lost knowledge is, for Badi, almost the equivalent of a holy duty.

Bashir Ali
b. Mehriz, 1947

Bashir Ali's work has been published by the Polisario's Ministry of Culture in an effort to preserve the best in Hassaniyah poetry but he is still very much in the oral tradition. His story of how he came to poetry – a boy who listened to older poets, instinctively connected with them and slowly got to know their poems until he could produce his own – is one which most poets will recognise.

Bashir is proud of the distinctiveness of the Hassaniyah tradition. Like many people I spoke to about this, he reckons it to be more difficult as a form than classical Arabic poetry citing as proof the requirement to find a rhyme at the end of each half line as well as at the end of each line.

Saharawi poetry reconciles the traditional and the modern. The poems of today are composed in the same form as those from before the 1975 war but, as Bashir told me, the theme was very different. They were poems drawn from individual experience: love of the land or of a lover. Now, as in Bashir's own work –

praise poems for national heroes, poems to encourage, uplift or celebrate - poetry is much more about the collective experience. His poems speak of solidarity; written in response to the works of individuals (the activists of Gdeim Izik or the legendary activists of the past), they make the act of poetry and of hearing poetry part of a collective resistance. They stem from the belief that 'the cause,' as Bashir says, 'is a general one.'

Beyibouh El-Haj Mohamed Molud

b. in Lem Hadjib, Sagia Valley, 1928 or 29

If I tried to explain what I was doing to strangers on the camps, I would say, 'I am a poet,' and then when they did not understand that, perhaps because he was the first poet I met, I'd add, 'a poet. Like Beyibouh.' That each time I was met with the same smiling response of immediate recognition shows the affection in which poetry in general and Beyibouh in particular are held on the camps. 'His poems are very difficult,' people would tell me, as high praise.

Beyibouh was born in Spanish Sahara in the late 1920s (before anyone was interested in remembering or recording birthdays) and lived through many important stages of Western Sahara's history: from European occupation, to resistance and Moroccan invasion, through exile and diplomatic stalemate. On the relations with the Spanish during the colonial era, he is relatively positive. There were, he says, four points of agreement between the colonisers and the Jama'a, the colonial constituted 'tribal elders' of the various Hassaniyah speaking peoples. As Beyibouh saw it, they agreed to the Spanish presence on the condition that there would be no inter-marriage; the Saharawi were not forced into Spanish service, paid no taxes and were allowed to keep their own arms. Mainly, they continued their lives as Bedouin herding camels and goats.

Three of Beyibouh's grandparents were poets and from a young age he began composing and reciting poetry as well. Yet, among the Saharawi there is no concept of caste poets as in other oral cultures and he does not consider his family's poetic heritage to confer on him any special status. His primary identification is as a Bedouin. 'If there is anyone who missed the civilised world and expensive things, that's me!' he explained. He had his goats and his camels and he wandered the paths of the desert, following the rain. 'I never liked to be in cities and big towns,' he told me.

The armed struggle started with the example of and, for the movement's leaders, practical experience abroad with liberation movements in neighbouring countries. When the Moroccans invaded and the Saharawi organised themselves to resist the new invader, everything changed. In the chaos and carnage, Beyibouh (who would have been nearly 50) and his family escaped to the newly established refugee camps taking very little with them. Poetry changed too. After 1975 it went, in Beyibouh's words, 'hand-in-hand with arms'. The poems they composed in those years broadcast what the army were doing, encouraged the population and were themselves a 'weapon that poets used to reveal the true face of Morocco. Poetry can cross the berm and fly across the sky. No guard can keep it away and no missile can destroy it.' With the growth of revolutionary consciousness, the abandonment of traditional tribal divisions and the new unity of armed struggle, it was, says Beyibouh, also a golden age for Saharawi poetry: 'the time of fighting and liberation was the time of poetry's flourishing'.

He believes that one must study poetry until it becomes 'part of the person', and listening to him, while sitting as a guest on the carpeted floor of his family's tent, with the clatter of tea cups on metal trays and the laughter of those around him, it is hard to tell the exact moment when he moves from talking to reciting. Beyibouh's poetry is a kind of refined talk and has (in its original at least) a distinctive, colloquial voice. One of his best known poems from that 'time of fighting' was the first poem he gave me, 'Dreimissa', an ode to the Land Rover. Once the only vehicle in the refugee camps, in its 'hornless' form (roof removed to mount a gun), the Land Rover became a symbol of the war of independence: a cheap DIY, re-commissioned vehicle that took on the might of the vastly better equipped Moroccan army. Many people I spoke to could recite lines from the poem. His poetry is funny, partisan and deeply loved and he has an infectious humour and magnetism about his person that is hard not to love too.

His first marriage was in 1952 and lasted till his wife's death, thirty years later. Remarried now, he says he is getting old and starting to forget things. Impeccably hospitable and warm, he welcomed me with an easy-going generosity, compliments and humour, showing an interest in me despite the fifty year gap of experience in our respective crafts.

The second time I met him, he gave me some of his more recent poems. They are the voice of an elder, intervening in contemporary debates. In 'To The Young People', there is a message of warning but not of despair. As he said to me: 'The poets of today grew up in the hands of the older generation and there is a continuity of what they have heard from their fathers and grandfathers'. However, despite the prestige afforded him by his life's achievements, he is clear that poetry is neither a career nor a means for personal glory. He is proudest when talking as a inheritor of a herding, nomadic tradition rather than as one of its most well-known poets: 'I have never in my life slept in a fancy place', he told me.

Hadjatu Aliat Swelm

b. Sagir Valley, Western Sahara , 1973

On my second visit to the camps, I was introduced to Hadjatu by Zeinab, a journalist and women's activist who runs a radio show addressing women's issues. Bendir drove us over to Hadjatu's place, but she was out fetching her son from school, so we walked into her unlocked house and sat in her front room to wait for her there.

She arrived and seemed happy to meet me. As a mother and refugee, she says that everyday concerns and problems take her away from poetry and she seemed almost relieved to have a couple of hours to bring out her notebooks and swap poetry and discuss ideas. Born in the Occupied Zone, Hadjatu wrote political poems, passing them to activists who would publish them on websites pseudonymously. However, one poem about sixty-six political prisoners interred in Morocco led to the Moroccan authorities discovering her identity. After that, she was subject to what she describes as 'pressure'. Her house was frequently raided, she was followed in the streets and eventually she was forced to leave. Since 1999, she has lived in Aosserd camp.

She believes in poetry's potential as a 'weapon' in the struggle, saying that, 'poetry is a gift that, despite the difference of languages and backgrounds, binds us together.' As well as the 'Gdeim Izik' poem published here, she also read me a poem about women activists in Smara in the Occupied Territories and another more general piece about women's part in the Saharawi struggle and I greatly regret that Mohamed and I did not have a chance to translate them. Talking about passing on the poem that had led to her persecution, she joked, 'I hope that there is a better way of getting these things to you'.

Hossein Mo'ulud Mohamed Salem

b. Moha Salim, 1952

'Poetry,' says Hossein Mo'olud is a 'means to carry on the struggle'. At around 20 years old, Hossein became friends with a man from whom he learned poetry. This poetry mentor was not a family member and the way Hossein describes him – words translated to me as 'striking, handsome, entertaining' – suggests that the making of this friendship was one of those significant moments of late adolescence that shift our way of thinking and form our adult character. This personal revolution, coming as it did in the early 1970s, must have chimed resonantly with the political situation around him. Hossein became involved in the early Saharawi movement for self-determination, playing his youthful part in the 1971 Zimla *Intifada*. Soon he was also learning and practicing poetry.

Born in herding country, Hossein's family had settled in the capital, L'Ayoune by the time the Moroccans invaded. They did not stay around to wait for them. As King Hassan's army was sweeping across the country, leaving a trail of destruction in their wake, the family took what they could and left on foot, in two separate groups. One part of them was attacked on their way but Hossein's party escaped safely to the newly formed camps of Tindouf, where he still lives.

His mentor was in hospital at the time of the invasion and stayed in Western Sahara. Hossein heard no more of him until a couple of years ago when he heard the family's name in connection with a tragedy where a number of people died in one of the desert's sudden unexpected spells of darkness. Hossein managed to track down his friend, who was still alive, and they met again in March 2014 in Ponta Delgada in the Portuguese Azores islands.

I met Hossein twice. Traditionally dressed in a *dara*, he had his poetry written on paper. He gave me a large selection of his political verse. He patiently explained to me his view of the injustice the Saharawis have suffered and are suffering, something that is central to his work. His poetry often involves extended metaphors as in 'Haima', glorifying the tent as a symbol of resistance, or, in a poem not included here, a long praise-poem of a traditional female hairstyle as coded praise for Western Sahara itself.

Mahmoud Hadri

b. Aossard camp, 1982

Mahmoud graduated with a BA in Law from university in Algeria and is now employed by the Polisario Ministry of Culture, in charge of the national library. We drove over to L'Ayoune camp to meet him at his house, which he was in the process of extending to accommodate a new arrival. A toddler played while we talked.

Of all the poets I met, Mahmoud was the only poet who writes his poetry in classical Arabic but he was born into a family of poets who composed poetry in the language which they spoke, Hassaniya. He explained to me that Arabic 'did not plant deep roots' among the Saharawi for a number of reasons:

1. The Spanish did not build schools at all in Western Sahara so even those who were settled were not formally educated. For most people, the only contact with written Arabic was through the language of the Koran. It was not much part of the spoken language.

2. Although most of the Polisario intellectuals and leadership were educated abroad and often in Arabic-speaking countries, back home they focussed on developing Hassaniyah poetry as this was the language that the masses understood. Classical Arabic was 'like a stranger in the society'.

Hassiniyah poetry, however, is (like most Saharawi endeavours) severely repressed in the homeland, suffers from a lack of resources to publish in the camps and Arabic publishers have shown little interest in promoting minority languages or dialects. Thus, Mahmoud who had an interest in literature from an early age, has decided to contribute to the struggle in Arabic.

With an increasing number of Saharawi attending university, there is a bigger audience for his poetry among his own people and in Arabic he can reach out to a potential readership across the Arab world. Yet Arab interest is still far from guaranteed. Unlike the Palestinian cause which, being an inter-faith conflict, has the overwhelming support of the Muslim world, the Saharawi struggle against their fellow Muslim occupiers has often been dismissed as a socialist, 'eastern bloc' affair. But in the battle for hearts and minds, Morocco cannot only claim Arab solidarity, its royal family also has the support of other Arab – and indeed world – monarchies. Feudal overlords tend to back each other up. Arab monarchs are understandably not interested in promoting the cause of independence and liberation from a fellow Arab king and media in the Arab world must follow certain interests. Mahmoud suspects this is why it has been hard for him to find an Arab website to publish his political essays. He hopes that, unable to garner political support in the Arab world, the Saharawi may be able to reach people culturally and his poetry is an attempt to do that. In 2011, Algiers was the Arab Capital of Culture and Mahmoud published his book 'Pains of the Ocean' [Polisario Ministry of Culture] for an Arabic literature event.

Yet Mahmoud is quick to recognise that Arabic poetry is just one part of the struggle. Especially in the Occupied Territories themselves, he informed me, even the act of composing poems in Hassaniya is an important act of resistance. For a long time there had been limited contact between the camps and the Occupied Territories because of absolute restrictions on travel and the fear of censorship or punishment. Families still to this day remain separated but there has been some limited granting of permits while the internet has provided a new ways to communicate across the Berm. Fear of reprisals keep Hassaniyah poetry from flourishing but poets pseudonymously use blogs and other means to spread their messages. On the camps, the Ministry of Culture was able to publish a book of a poet from inside the Occupied Territories. Hassaniyah poetry, says Mahmoud, is even more prevalent under occupation because the battle is at its heart a cultural one. 'Our culture and dialect,' he says, 'is our last weapon' in a place where there is an ongoing 'systematic Moroccanisation'. Especially for young people who have never known anything other than occupation, keeping Saharawi culture alive is vital for the struggle. Some of the poetry merely aims to preserve the idea of Saharawi culture and some is brave enough to address the political issues directly. However, as a poet living in the uncensored environment of the Tindouf refugee camps, Mahmoud has decided to devote himself to Arabic poetry, hoping to spread support for the cause across the Arab world.

Nadgem Said Oala
b. Aossard Camp, 1984

Born into a family of poets, Nadgem was born and educated in the camps up until the age of eleven when, like many Saharawi children before NATO's intervention in the insurgency against Muammar Gaddafi, he went to secondary school in Libya. Nadgem completed his education in Algeria, where he now attends university. As is clear in his poem 'For the Duty of the Saharawi Student Towards His Homeland', Nadgem believes that being a student carries with it a strong sense of responsibility.

I was introduced to Nadgem by my translator, Mohamed, who is a contemporary and a friend. Nadgem travelled over to Smara from Aosserd to meet me at the family compound where I was staying. Unusually among the young people I met, he wore the traditional *dara*. As it was getting later in the day, with the shadows lengthening and the heat dropped off a little, we sat on a carpet laid outside in the middle of the compound and discussed and shared poetry.

I found him a serious and intense young man, though with

his friends there was the usual good humour common to Saharawi interaction. For someone of his generation, never having visited the homeland, aged seven at the time of the ceasefire and knowing only the prolonged stalemate in which the Western Saharan cause has floundered, there is the question of where activism goes next. The young people I mixed with were internet savvy, using online activism to further the cause. Many spoke good English and were keen to learn more, creating blogs and videos with English subtitles to show to the world the protests and the conditions of the exiles. Yet, there seemed to be a feeling among them that not all of their generation share their commitment and are accepting too readily the status quo of exile, seeking out business opportunities rather than pursuing the cause of independence.

Nadgem elaborated to me that university studies must serve something bigger, something in which all Saharawi are part. His poetry is suffused with a strong sense of political commitment. He started organising poetry readings on campus and, on days of national celebration, he arranges poetry events to bring together as many as possible of the Saharawi students who are dispersed across Algeria's universities. Back in the camps for the summer, he stages recitals for the new young poets to bring their work back to the people.

In this situation, Nadgem says, the new generation of poets, must create a new poetry for the times. Poetry, for him, is a response to the people's needs and problems of the moment. During the war, the revolutionary concerns were immediate and a part of daily life. Now, perhaps, with no end in sight, the thinking must be longer term. However, it is not only in his dress that he respects the Hassaniyah traditions. His poetry is composed with the structures of traditional poetry and he readily acknowledges that moving forward means knowing where you come from.

When I questioned him, he admitted that he has written some love poems and more light-hearted work but his main object is political. He is attempting to write a Saharawi *Iliad*, with each section 40 lines long, one line for each year of the struggle. He writes mainly in Hassaniya but he has written in Classical Arabic as well.

Despite the problems and the obstacles before them, he believes that the youth are about to explode, and he dreams to be able to use poetry for the cause of the nation. 'I write almost every day,' he says. 'My heart is full of things I want to contribute to the cause.'

Jacob Mundy & Stephen Zunes

Jacob Mundy is an assistant professor of peace and conflict studies at Colgate University. Stephen Zunes is a professor of politics and international studies at the University of San Francisco, where he also directs the Middle Eastern Studies Programme.

Together they have coauthored several publications, including *Western Sahara: War, Nationalism, and Conflict Irresolution* (Syracuse University Press 2010).

Mustafa El-Kattab

Mustafa El-Kattab is the Senior Saharawi Minister of Foreign Affairs and the former Saharawi Ambassador in Syria.

PART THREE

Original poems transliterated from Hassaniya
to Arabic.

(reading in order from the 'back' of the book)

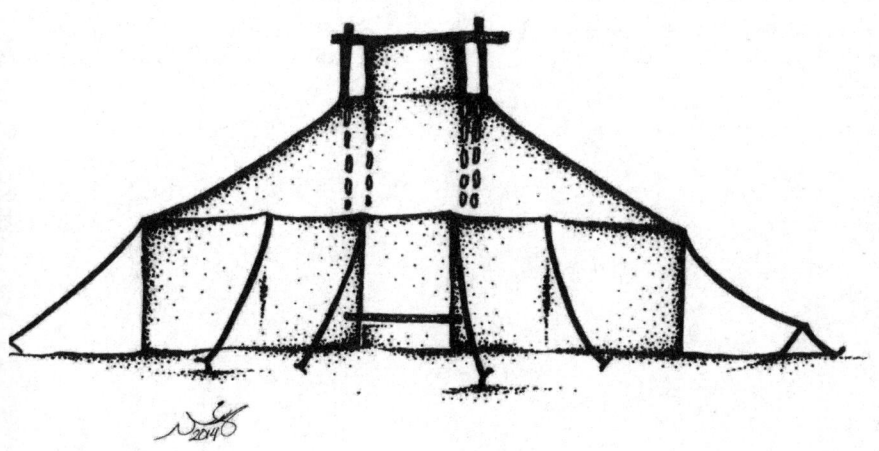

To the Activists of Gdeim Izik
Nadgem Said

إلى مناضلي كديم ازيك
الناجم سعيد غلا

نعتو للعالم بافتخار	الثوار لفكديم ازيك
مارتنا و امارة لحرار	عنا شعب امتين و هذيك
المغرب بالجور و الاجرام	ثارو فكديم ازيك و قام
و المؤبد و العالم حار	و اصدر فيهم حكم الاعدام
الدولي نزهم من عار	فيهم عاقب فات النظام
السادس زعيم الاشرار	بطش المغرب و اخزيو الفام

الثوار لفكديم ازيك

ما يعرف حكم و لاهو قد	بسمن حق يحاكمهم حد
ما يعرف شي ما هو لنكار	الحكم و حكمو مستبد
فيهم ياسر شين و مطيار	بسم الحكم العسكري هد
بناي الثورة بافتخار	غير ابقاو ابفخر مسند

الثوار لفكديم ازيك

192

A Gift for the Saharawi Soldier Nadgem Said

هدية إلى المقاتل الصحراوي
الناجم سعيد غلا

يا المقاتل يومك لطوف   بالمجد على فم كلاشك

ظاهر فيه النصر و معروف   ليكد يواسي رشاشك

و يا المقاتل حسم الكفاح   فاصل فيه الشعب بسلاح

فيديك انت يطلس لسراح   للوطن بافعال كلاشك

ذيك الزينة بيها لصاح   يجنب لعدو نقاشك

بيه ليعرف فالحرب شطاح   منو بفعايل رشاشك

يا المقاتل يومك لطوف

و يا المقاتل ظرك المصير   قرو و اصنع للشعب اخير

صنعك لوطانك بالتحرير   لترابك و ارضك و افاراشك

لاحق وقتك لعليه ادير   فوق اكتافك حل كلاشك

و توكل فالحي القدير   ما نافع شي غير غراشك

بقوالك و افعالك لتسير   بيها للمجد افمعاشك

و الى مت تعود على خير   شهادة منشور فراشك

يا المقاتل يومك لطوف   بالمجد على فم كلاشك

ظاهر فيه النصر و معروف   ليكد يواسي رشاشك

و انتوما يا الجامعيات   كيفت ذاك انتومات فات
عاد اعليكم حمل ارادات   الشعب و روزو لفادة
أطبيبات و معليمات   منكم مديورة ليشادة
بالعلم وصلتو مرتبات   نعتتكم فالعالم قادة
و انعتو عنكم لاجيات   فريدات النوع و عادة
فيكم صنيع المعجزات   و افذاك انتوما عبادة

يا الجامعي مطروح عليك

و بكل اختصار انت قل   يا الجامعي نابض فالشعب
طالب منك عنك تنصب   سلاح العلم بلفادة
ذي هي لوطان على درب   ريح النصر اللا تتقادى
و تحاني صنيعك و الحب   للوطن دين و عبادة
و افهم ذاك و قوم و جرب   فوطانك عيش السيادة

يا الجامعي مطروح عليك   حمل استرجاع السيادة
من مذال الشعب يحانيك   كيف تحانيك القيادة

The Duty of the University Student Towards His Homeland
by Nadgem Said

واجب الطالب الجامعي نحو وطنه
الناجم سعيد غلا

يا الجامعي مطروح عليك	حمل استرجاع السيادة
من مذال الشعب يحانيك	كيف تحانيك القيادة
و الجامعي حرك لقلام	و اكتب عن شعبك لا تلتام
و شمزي علم بلا مرام	لعادت ما فيه افادة
كوم بفكرك و اوصف لالام	و المعانات و تكادة
عن لرض عليها من لسقام	لمنكل بيها و العادة
حد مرقها لاهي يلتام	و امنين العزم و ليرادة
لمشى بيها شهيدك تام	و امشات افذاك الشهادة

يا الجامعي مطروح عليك

و العلم اللي عندك فالراس	شعبك فاصل فيه و ليحساس
بيه انت مطلوب و بلباس	ثوب النصر و لا تتمادة
عن ذاك و خليك ابجناس	الشعب و حاول لفادة
قيمة لوطان بلا مقياس	سنين الغزو و لحمادة
و انشر علومك بين الناس	و اطرح حلول السيادة

يا الجامعي مطروح عليك

كافي يا الجامعي عن فم	فاللوجو شعبك عايش هم
العربة و البعد و لطم	عن لعدو ماطل و تمادى
و احنا فالتشريد و لالم	و لسابق ذاك من ابادة
ذرك اص ما نافع ندم	لعدو شايف فيك اشادة
بالنصر و عايش منك غم	و اطلب من ذاك الزيادة
و اصنع مصير الشعب و لم	الشمل ابلرض بهوادة

يا الجامعي مطروح عليك

195

Tishuash
Badi

التيشواش
بادي

مات الماضي سبحان الحي
عييت نشوفو ما هو فاي
كيف نبات على فم حسي
فالليل ينهول عنك عي
و الله ياللالك دهر اري
لفرقان الحية و شوي
فسرية من حي الى حي
قبل ظهور الشمس على ري
ينظرها ما خافيه ودي
و اتاي على ما فيه الطي
قيق بعيد اهلو من لحفي
و افراش حذا بلد الشي
عنك ما تتفقد يا خي

الدايم ما غلى منو زي
حاضر ما حاضر فيه اواش
بل ثراه ماسيه فراش
بهانيس و حس الخشاش
زرعو ما فات طلس لعراش
ثاني ما عينك فالتنباش
تفاق مراكيو تتناش
العين المعالم فراش
منها فملاس و لا فحراش
من تورطة وللا من ماش
ماه قليل و حطبو قشقاش
و اعظام حذا ذاك افراش
هذا من شي لذيذ نعاش

Aminatou Haidar
Bashir Ali

أمنتو حيدار
لبشير أعلي

لعليات الى دفعو بعد
ما لاهي يلحق منهم حد
حب الشعب من اجلو ضحات
و عطات الروح و لا خلات
و سوى بغيو ما بيه سخات
و سخات براحتها و مشات
منتو ذا لوسات و رات
فالرجال قبل لعليات
قد خلق فالدهر اللي فات
أنا بعد و لاهي تفتات
و لا قط عليه مردة جات

و الرجال فشي ذا نبتو
سير نعالة لمنتو
بالمال و لولاد و لمنات
شي مالكتو يسوى نبتو
فامر التحرير و وظفتو
مهلا ياك اللا شفتو
ريتو لو مثيل شقلتو
قولو وللا بيه سمعتو
وللا حاضر فيه بحثتو
ما نللا ما قط جبرتو
و شهدتو بما علمتو

197

Activists
Bashir Ali

المناضلين
لبشير أعلي

عاقب ذا من معطى لنفاس
و البط على الراس فلحباس
اللي لاهي يخون من الناس
ما هو فالي يا كواني
و لساني و بلد وجداني
ما يغلق بلدو شي شي ثاني
لي يساويه لسوى لعطاني
شعبي و اوطاني و اقراني
نخون وجودي يا كواني
راشي محدور مع شاني
يشوي موتاه لحجاني

و الدم و لعرق و السجون
و الجر فلحجار بلقرون
اللا مكتوب عليه يخون
قع نخون أهلي و اوطاني
و الكيان اللي بيه نكون
فالكون و لا عندي فالكون
فيه الكون يتم اللا دون
نقبظ و نخون اثري مجنون
نبقى فكرون بلا مضمون
محدور و محقور و مهيون
بنخون اللا راهو ملعون

198

الجيش
الخضرة المبروك

شور ملك اهلو ما تعطيه	يا لغزو لماشي هباط
شاف عنو موحال عليه	فات جاه الروم ليتباط
حد قاعد فوق اكرسيه	ما تجيبو كثرة لعياط
قال شعب قليل و نغزيه	دار تاجو فيه التخطاط
قام هاجم بالعنف عليه	غير دار الجيش احتياط
شال تاجو و كفى كرسيه	طاعنو مليك الرباط
ذاك عند الجبهة راعيه	و كل شي جابو بيه حتاط
هازمك و الجو كفطيه	عاد بيه مكسر لرباط
دعم ريقن و العالق فيه	و حقرك فانواع التخطاط
جيش يوم عقيد نواصيه	و فشلك فآلات الدمار
خش خش الغار اراعيه	فم غزوك يشبه لحبار
سيدكم فالدهر ابديه	ما تلا يانساها لحمار
قال شعب قليل و نغزيه	و لا تلا يتخمم فافكار
يالله ذا الجيش تنجيه	و اللي بيه الجيش المغوار

The Berm
Al Khadra

الجدار
الخضرة المبروك

الملك   الربط   بناه   و لعندو كامل دارو فيه
يغير الجيش دخل موراه   و قبظ بيديه لعينو فيه

Resist
Mahmoud Khadri

قاوم
محمود خطري

إن العيون من العذاب تعتصر
كسر قيودك فالصحراء تنتظر
مدينة لو ترى في طرفها حور
كالطلح نحن فلا
ضعف و لا خور
جرح العيون له القلوب تنفطر
و القلب باك و دمع العين ينهمر
و ابشر بنصر فإن
الشعب مقتدر
و سل نجوم العلا يجيبك القمر
و اعط دماءك فالجلاد يحتضر
إنا سئمنا من الأراء و الخطب
فثورة الشعب لا
تخلو من الغضب

قاوم جراحك لا ماء و لا شجر
جمد دموعك لا وقت نضيعه
إن العيون التي نبكي لها وجعا
إن الغواة و إن يستنزفو دمنا
يا صاح لا تقل ماتت مطامحنا
تبكي عيونك و الجراح توغرها
و افتح عمورية
الصحراء معتصما
فاركب وعور الدنا
ذلل مخاطرها
يا صاح لا تترك الجلاد يجلدها
يا قلعة المجد
ثوري اليوم و اقتربي
و علقي فوق كل خيمة غضبا

Landscape
Badi

الأرض
بادي

يا عيني عاقب لبادوة
راعي لك ذيك الحدادة
يا عيني عاقب ذا اللي فات
تنقفوف و بعد اللي رات
و عاقب يا كراعي بالليعات
هذا راعيه من التنعات
اللي يا عيني و كراعي
الدوقج راعيه و وُاعي

و لبعد من ترابك وهاي
و قرونة و دغد النقاي
من بعد الدوقج و قليبات
لخلاق املي من لوقوف
عن لجواد الليك مكروف
عاد اقرب حمدو للرؤوف
و اخلاقي منكم ذاك يشوف
لجواد و راعي تنقفوف

Landscape II
Badi

الأرض
بادي

و لبعد من ترابك وهاي
و قرونة و دغد النقاي
لمبروكين و لروي مسكين
هاذي تنيرقات الدواي
قلابة لميلح و ابراي

يا عيني عاقب لبادوة
راعي لك ذيك الحدادة
شوف لذوك النوراشيين
شوفيه و شوفي عن يمين
يالعين و شوفي عن يمين

Advice
Badi

نصيحة
بادي

قلت شي فايدو ذاك لبيه
أرخس تحت ايدو شي يعطيه

حد ارخس قولو لو من قد
ما هي شينة شن الا حد

Frente Polisario
Beyibou Al Haj

جبهة البوليساريو
بيبوه ولد الحاج

الجبهة قبظت مقعدها   فالعالم و اعترف بيها
على عينين الحاسدها   و على عينين الباغيها
فالميدان اللا مول مراد   و لحاسدها قاع الى عاد
و يقاني مجموع الحساد   للدولة داير يثنيها
ماهو بأنيها و افطن زاد   اقليل ذاك لعاطيها

يتركها تقبظ مقعدها   فالعالم و اعترف بيها
على عينين الحاسدها   و على عينين الباغيها

لحاسدها من طبع الحال   ما جاها فايام النضال
و لا جاب النساء و الاطفال   قوة الاعداء اطاويها
و لا جاب لها قد اللي قال   كانو لرواح يهجيها
و لا شاف الشهداء الابطال   ما خلاه لاهو فيها
غير منين نكزت رجال   و جابت شعب امين ايديها
اللي ذاك قبظ مكانو   فمراكزها و اساميها
و لحاسدها باحر كانو   يكرهها و للا يبغيها

الجبهة قبظت مقعدها   فالعالم و اعترف بيها
على عينين الحاسدها   و على عينين الباغيها

شفت الدولة ما كونها   يا الحسود و ما قوننها
و شفت ملي ما هدنها   امنين تسافي عينيها
و للتجارب ما دونها   و مباديها شفت شفيها
لعل يحجلك عنها   فتعسريها و تعريبها
ما تعرف ذاك لعانيها   و تعرف ذاك لعان عليها
يغير اللي ما هو منها   وللا خاتر عنها جيها
يخليها فماكنها   أباش الله مخليها
مساعت قبظت مقعدها   فالعالم و اعترف بيها
على عينين الحاسدها   و على عينين الباغيها

هذي مجموعات النظام   اللي وافي فيكم لكلام
و فايديكم لكلاش الى صام   اتسييها و تصينها
ما تعرف يكون التقدام   شور عدو تنتقم منها
و هذي حجة من يوم لقام   الجيش الشعبي تاقنها
كان اص عبارة ليام   تحسنها ولا تخشنها

الشبيبة عيب عليها   و لاني بالعيب معاينها
يغير علاه اراضيها   تعريها ولا ترهنها

To the Young People
Beyibou Al Haj

إلى الشباب
بييبوه ولد الحاج

الشبيبة عيب عليها و لاني بالعيب معاينها
يغير اعلاه اراضيها تعريها وللا ترهنها
يالشباب لمانك موصوف فالترقي عن تخلوف
شايف لشجار تموت وقوف فماكنها ما كونها
وقوف القلابة صفوف ما تتحيد عن وطنها
وشقال الانسان الملوف عاطي فارضيتو ثمنها
يمشي عنها باسباب الخوف ما مات عليها ما شينها
الثورة يوم علنتوها ما عزيمتكم تثنوها
سابق لهداف تحقوها أبكرامتها و امنها
و اخير اليوم تجدوها و يعود الجيس مدشنها
و اهل المناطق غيثوها لعاد لباقي شي منها
راهب كل نهار عدوها ينشفها و يرغنها

الشبيبة عيب عليها و لاني بالعيب معاينها
يغير علاه اراضيها تعريها وللا ترهنها

هذي مجموعات البيظان للي مزدادة فالميدان
و أصالة من نطفة شجعان قوة لعدو ما يشطنها
إغمبان اولاد إغمبان تشبه علي كاد انها
ما يحزمها يوم الحمان حس الوطيس يمزنها
تزكن فانحاي البلدان هي شنهو لمزقننها
تحاني جيوش الجبان إلين تحوش معادنها
هذا ماهو حال الشبان لعيان اللي هي منها

الشبيبة عيب عليها و لاني بالعيب معاينها
يغير علاه اراضيها تعريها وللا ترهنها

207

Mohammed Bassiri
Leader, Harakat Tahrir- 'disappeared' 1970

Acknowledgements

Thanks are due to all those who helped make this project happen. To the interpreters I worked with for the tireless work on my behalf: Chaka, Lejlifa, Mohamed and Zorgan. To the Polisario Ministry of Culture and to Limam and Sidi at the Polsario Mission in London for arranging the trips and setting up the meetings with the poets: I am extremely grateful for the willingness and efficiency in seeing to all my needs. To Mimi, Zorgan and family for the excellent hospitality and to all the people I met on the camps. To all the poets who have contributed to this book; I hope I have done justice to your words.

To Kit at Influx for backing this project, the support you have provided and for the editorial and other invaluable work necessary to complete it, and to Gary too. To all the people who donated to fund the project. To Becky and David at Olive Branch Arts for bringing me along on the first trip and introducing me to the Saharawi people and getting me deeper into the cause. To Becky, Bobby, Emma and Izzy for the companionship and collaboration on my first trip to the camps. To Jacob and

Stephen for contributing an introduction to this book and for the brilliant scholarly research which has informed so much of my understanding of the conflict. To Mustafa for his introduction to the poetry. And finally to Nora for the Budapest writing residencies and for everything you have given me over this last year.

- Sam Berkson

Mohamed Sulaiman

Mohamed Sulaiman was born in Dakhla Camp, south-west Algeria in 1986. He studied English literature and Civilisation at Batna University, Algeria. He now works as an illustrator and a translator in the Saharawi Refugee Camps, Algeria.

Mohamed worked with Sam Berkson to produce the literal translations from Hassaniya to Arabic to English. Mohamed also provided transcriptions of the Hassaniya poetry in Arabic that can be read at the back of this book, and the illustraions throughout.

Sam Berkson

Sam Berkson was born in the London Borough of Bromley in 1982. He grew up in Hertfordshire and Cambridgeshire. He is the author of *Life in Transit* (Influx Press, 2012), *Dusk Steals the Daylight* (Fishbar, 2013) and the words in Lorenzo Vitturi's photobook, *Dalston Anatomy* (SPBH, 2013).

He now lives in Hackney, London and is the host of live poetry events for Hammer & Tongue and the Re:Versed show on NTS radio. The author's profits from this book will be donated to Olive Branch Arts who intend to set up a fund for Saharawi artists living in the Tindouf refugee camps.

This book was made possible by the following supporters:

Jack Warner	Euan Monaghan
Valerie Caless	James Gooch
Mark Beechill	Michael Noble
Catherine de Lange	Ross Motley
Darren Chetty	Poetcurious
Paul Hawkins	Richard Airlie
Rachel Weston	Charlotte Bence
Simon Evans	Rebecca Marcus
Becky Hall	Rachel Marcus
Vikki Brackenbury	Joey Hasson
Trinity John	Colin Griffiths
Emma Brown	Sarah Abbey
Gareth E Rees	Nick Wilsdon
Owen Booth	Jules Arthur

Linda Mannheim

Sarah Berkson

A F Harrold

Leila Bawa

Guy Shennan

Roggy Drouinaud

Helen Moss & Jonny Garelick

Alex Balkwill

Michael Berkson

Jan Klaerke Thogersen

Diana Pinkett

Aki Schilz

Our deepest thanks to each and every one of these *Settled Wanderers* backers, without your support at the beginning of this project we wouldn't have been able to make the book.

Glossary of terms

Hassaniya:
Arabic dialect of the Western Sahara, spoken by most Saharawi and Mauritanians

Berm Wall:
The military wall built around the Occupied Zones

Liberated Zones:
Small area of Western Sahara under Polisario control, to the east of the Berm

Dara:

Traditional Saharawi male attire; a full robe

Haima:

Saharawi tent

L'Ayoune:

Capital of Western Sahara

المناطق المحتلة

Occupied Zones:
The area Morocco controls, fromerly Spanish Sahara

جبهة البوليساريو

Polisario Front:
The Saharawi government in exile

قديم ازيك

Gdeim Izik:
The site of a large protest in 2010

Milfa:

Traditional Saharawi female attire, covering head and body

Tindouf:

City in South-Western Algeria, near to the refugee camps.

Waleia:

A province, used to refer to one of the four refugee camps

INFLUX
PRESS

Influx Press is an independent publisher specialising in writing about place.

We publish challenging, controversial and alternative work that blurs genres, producing site-specific fiction, poetry and creative non-fiction.

www.influxpress.com